SWIM WITH THE
SHARKS

Without Being Eaten Alive

—————◆—————

HARVEY MACKAY

Foreword by Kenneth Blanchard

SPHERE BOOKS LIMITED

SPHERE BOOKS LTD

Published by the Penguin Group
27 Wrights Lane, London W8 5TZ, England
Viking Penguin Inc., 40 West 23rd Street, New York, New York 10010, USA
Penguin Books Australia Ltd, Ringwood, Victoria, Australia
Penguin Books Canada Ltd, 2801 John Street, Markham, Ontario, Canada L3R 1B4
Penguin Books (NZ) Ltd, 182–190 Wairau Road, Auckland 10, New Zealand

Penguin Books Ltd, Registered Offices: Harmondsworth, Middlesex, England

First published in Great Britain by Michael Joseph Ltd 1988
Published by Sphere Books Limited 1989
1 3 5 7 9 10 8 6 4 2

Made and printed in Great Britain by
Richard Clay Ltd, Bungay, Suffolk

DEDICATION

Two incredible men have been mentors to me throughout the years. My late father, Jack Mackay, was an exceptional journalist whose invaluable life-lessons have always guided me.

He left giant footsteps in which I've tried to walk. Rudy Miller, my father-in-law, is a one-of-a-kind entrepreneur, gentleman, and humanitarian whose genuine zest for life has energized our entire family. If there's a better business-man anywhere in the country, I've yet to meet him, and I still can't believe my good fortune in becoming his 'son' when I fell in love with his daughter.

FOREWORD

If you've just opened this book not knowing what to expect, you're in for a big treat. *Swim with the Sharks Without Being Eaten Alive* is not one of those useless collections of wornout business school wisdom, but an extraordinary treasure chest of information *you can apply immediately* to your business, your life, your relationships, and your goals. I have mixed feelings saying this because one part of me wants everyone to learn from the insights, genius, and creativity I've come to love about Harvey Mackay, while another part wants to hoard the information for myself. In striving to build my own track record, I'm convinced if I were the only person around who had this book I'd lap the field. I know you will not want your competition to get their hands on this wonderful book.

What's so special about this book? Plenty! Harvey Mackay has put together a collection of unforgettable life-lessons — quick, to-the-point parables and principles that will be invaluable to the novice and the veteran alike at any point in their business or personal lives. You're going to have fun comparing your favorite lessons with those of others who have read the book, whether they be business colleagues, friends, or family members.

What are my favorite lessons? Their titles alone will give you a taste for the vivid, common-sensical wisdom presented here:

- *Smile and Say No Until your Tongue Bleeds.*

- *Make Decisions with Your Heart, and What You'll End Up with Is Heart Disease.* Something I've known all along but couldn't put into words.

1

- *The Best Way to Chew Someone Out*. When he absolutely has to take someone to the woodshed, Harvey prefers to hand them the paddle and let them do it themselves. He seats them in the boss's chair and asks, 'All right, Jack, what would you say if you were me?' I've tried it a few times and it works better than a One-Minute Reprimand, but don't tell anybody.

- *66 Things You Ought to Know About Your Customers*. Everyone talks about sticking close to the customer, but Harvey Mackay does it. He keeps a file on every customer in which he requires his salespeople to answer 66 questions about that customer – everything from their college alma mater to their favorite hobby to their spouse's and children's names and accomplishments. Harvey knows more about his customers than they know about themselves . . . and certainly more than the competition does! You'll love the 'Mackay 66.'

- *Helping Your Kids Beat the Odds*. The chapter that takes this extraordinary book out of the realm of the 'business book' and makes it a book to share with your kids, of any age, touching every part of their lives. Mackay even has one rule to suggest to kids: *Make believe your parents are right some of the time*.

You might be wondering why you should listen to Harvey Mackay. Who's he? Well, he's a wise man – a super success. He's a man who:

- As a volunteer, served as the catalyst for a phenomenal community effort that culminated in the building of the $75 million Hubert H. Humphrey Metrodome in Minneapolis. He also has raised millions of dollars for everything from the American Cancer Society to sending the University of Minnesota Band to China.

- As a businessman, is the owner of a $35 million envelope manufacturing company that is a marketing and profitability standard-setter for the industry.

- As a loyal alumnus, talked Lou Holtz into coming to Minnesota to coach and turn around the Gophers' football program.

2

And in a decisive coup, he raised $6 million in a matter of days for a ticket buyout that kept the Twins major league baseball team in Minnesota.

Fortune magazine called Harvey Mackay 'Mr Make-Things-Happen.' *USA Today* said, 'Mackay's style is major league.' A Minnesota newspaper referred to Harvey Mackay as 'The Ultimate Volunteer.' Lou Holtz, now the Notre Dame football coach, claims, 'When I came up here [Twin Cities] and the wind-chill factor was about fifty degrees below zero, Harvey sold me six refrigerators.' All this, and Harvey Mackay's goals in life are: to be a good husband, a good father, a good businessman, and an active participant in the community.

Harvey Mackay has done it all, and he has given us a chronicle of the success strokes and survival tactics learned over three decades, that have lead to many accomplishments. But read the book, and get better at whatever you do – the Mackay way. You'll enjoy life more, and you might be surprised to find your most extravagant dreams becoming realities.

Thanks, Harvey!

– Kenneth Blanchard
Co-Author
The One Minute Manager

ACKNOWLEDGMENTS

Many people have helped me with *SWIM WITH THE SHARKS*. If I've learned just one thing from writing it, it's that I could not have done it alone.

My very special thanks go to my sister, Margie Resnick, who has been my sounding board and project assistant for over 20 years.

Adrian Zackheim, Senior Editor at William Morrow, improved the manuscript immeasurably. I enjoyed his professionalism, his poise under pressure, and his friendship.

Everyone at Morrow has been helpful. I'd especially like to thank Larry Hughes, Al Marchioni, Sherry Arden, Tom Consolino, Susan Halligan, Lela Rolontz, Lisa Queen and Will Schwalbe. At Hearst, Boyd Griffin was a vital ally.

So many other people were involved in the creation of this book that I'd like to elaborate on their special contributions, but I'm told that a book cannot consist of acknowledgments alone. Nonetheless, I am grateful to the following people for their part in *SHARKS*: My agent Jonathon Lazear, Marc Jaffe, Ron Beyma, Marilyn Carlson Nelson, Vickie Abrahamson, Lynne Lancaster, Martin Levin, Dave Mona, Nancy Doran, Carol Pine, Barry McCool and David Martin.

Ken Blanchard provided his keen wisdom and book publishing expertise throughout the process. I'm grateful for his thoughtful forward, and I'm indebted to Ken for his friendship and support.

Most of all, I'm grateful to my wife, Carol Ann, whose intelligence, creativity and support have helped me in countless ways in the writing and preparation of *SHARKS*. I could not have done it without her. And thanks and love to my children, David, Mimi and JoJo, who provided the perspective for so much of this book, especially the chapter, *HELPING YOUR KIDS BEAT THE ODDS*.

And one last thanks to the people at Mackay Envelope, who swim with the sharks daily, and who have provided me with the experiences that are the foundation of this book – and our success.

CONTENTS

Chapter 1

'I'D LIKE 15,000 TICKETS FOR TONIGHT'S GAME, PLEASE'

◆

The fifteen minutes of fame that the late Andy Warhol promised each of us came to me in the spring of 1984. I was the point man in a nationally publicized effort to outflank Calvin Griffith, the owner of the Minnesota Twins baseball team. Griffith wanted to sell his ball club to a group of Florida businesspeople who would have moved the Twins to Tampa. Another group, consisting of Twin Cities people, with which I was involved, wanted to keep the club there, under local ownership – and see to it that we didn't get caught up in a very expensive bidding war.

Unlike Calvin, we had a secret weapon: Bill Veeck.

In case you don't know who Bill Veeck is, he was the man who, in 1951, as owner of the hapless St. Louis Browns, staged an innocent-appearing promotion that so upset the baseball establishment – and so endeared him to baseball fans – that for as long as the game is played, he will be remembered as the man who 'sent a midget to bat.'

At three feet, seven inches and sixty-five pounds, Eddie Gaedel, ordinarily a vaudeville performer, gave the Browns one of their rare distinctions. He was the first and only certifiable midget to appear in a major-league baseball game. For the record, he walked on four straight pitches and upon reaching first base was replaced immediately by a pinch runner. True to form, the runner was stranded on third and the Browns lost the game. But from the uproar

Veeck had created you would have thought he'd called Babe Ruth a transvestite.

Veeck also operated five baseball clubs, three in the majors and two in the minors, won pennants, set major-league attendance records, was the promotional genius who helped innovate bat night, glove night, fan appreciation night, players' names on uniforms, exploding scoreboards, the ivy-covered walls of the Wrigley Field bleachers, the expansion of the major leagues, the unrestricted draft, and such yet-to-be-adopted proposals as interleague play.

In a word, he was a visionary. In another word, he was a maverick. My first contact with Veeck was simple enough. I picked up the phone and called him. Veeck prided himself on being totally accessible to anyone. Unlike most club owners, Veeck roamed the stands, schmoozing with his customers, instead of hiding out in a private box, à la Steinbrenner. Veeck had opinions on just about everything, and he loved to lay them on anyone who would listen.

As the situation in the Twin Cities began to unfold, I found myself calling Veeck almost daily. Here's what we were up against: Griffith had an escape clause in his stadium lease that permitted him to cancel if the Twins' attendance did not reach 4.2 million fans over a three-year period. Thanks to an inferior product, attendance over the previous two years had been so bad that by the end of the 1984 season the Twins would have had to draw 2.4 million to reach the 4.2 million total. However, if the total was reached, Griffith would be bound to his lease, and to Minnesota, for three more years.

Though he'd be free once again to leave after each three-year stint, he knew and we knew that once he had announced his desire to leave, the already disgruntled fans would turn on his shoddy product with a vengeance, and he would be forced to endure another three years of horrendous attendance and red ink.

So, unwilling to spend the money necessary to improve the team, he was determined to sell. Just as we were determined to see that the Twins hit 2.4 million in attendance in 1984. And he had only one group to sell to: us.

Our problem was that 2.4 million was an almost impossible goal. Veeck had set a major-league record that stood for fifteen years when he drew 2.8 million with a pennant-winning club in Cleveland. Less than a month into the 1984 season, it was clear the Minnesota Twins were going nowhere.

Confident that there was nothing anyone in Minneapolis or St. Paul could do to bind Griffith to his lease, in late April the Florida group endeared themselves to Griffith. They accomplished this by ridding him of a longtime antagonist, Gabe Murphy, when they bought Murphy's 43 percent minority interest in the club for $11 million.

Griffith then announced that he was open to all offers for his majority interest as long as they were for at least $50 million, which is what the pennant-contending Detroit club had just sold for. Calvin then sat back waiting for the bidding war to unfold between Tampa and Minnesota for the remaining stock.

What he hadn't counted on was the tenacity of the Twin Cities community and the long memory of Bill Veeck. Twenty-five years earlier, Veeck, as the owner of the Chicago White Sox, had voted at an American League meeting in favor of Griffith's move of the Washington Senators franchise to Minnesota. In exchange, Veeck felt he had an agreement from Griffith to support Veeck's bid for an expansion franchise in newly vacated Washington. To Veeck's mind, Griffith reneged on the deal when he voted for another group. It was an act Veeck would not forget. He devoted an entire chapter of his autobiography, *Veeck as in Wreck*, to Griffithian duplicity, a topic that also included another ancient wound inflicted years earlier when Griffith's uncle, Clark Griffith, supposedly reneged on a promise to let Veeck move the Browns' franchise to Baltimore.

15

What Veeck told me was that if we could mount a buyout of Twins tickets sufficient to boost 1984 attendance to 2.4 million, Griffith would cave in and sell to us *at our price*, knowing that if the club couldn't be packed off to Tampa, the fan resentment over his threatened move would be so great he couldn't afford to operate it any longer.

'Calvin can't take the pressure,' said Veeck. 'He couldn't take it when his family twisted his arm to vote the Washington franchise to their buddy, General Quesada, in 1961, and I am confident he won't fight once he sees you've got the financial muscle to back up a ticket buyout.'

Maybe. But it was a big gamble.

Griffith was getting cute and claiming that the 2.4 million had to be actual fans in attendance. Even giving away the tickets, we couldn't guarantee 2.4 million would actually pass through the turnstiles. Scarier still, the $6 million we raised from within the community wasn't necessarily enough money to guarantee 2.4 million attendance, live fans or not. Six million dollars would purchase only 1.4 million tickets. It might not be enough. We could never be sure how deep the well was, because unless another one million fans were willing to pay out of their own pockets – for tickets no better than the ones we were going to give away free – we'd fall short of the 2.4 million.

But I believed Veeck, who had been dreaming about getting even with the Griffiths for a quarter of a century and probably knew his old adversary better than anyone else on earth.

So I helped put together a group of influential supporters, held press conferences all over the state, set up offices to buy and distribute the tickets, and one day in May walked up to the Twins ticket booth in the Hubert H. Humphrey Metrodome with a cadre of reporters and announced to the young lady behind the counter, 'I'd like fifteen thousand tickets for tonight's game, please.'

From then on, it was easy sledding. I never really knew if

I could have gone back to our supporters for more money if we needed it, but what we had was enough to convince Calvin that the race was on and he'd either have to sell to us or watch his single greatest asset wash away in a sea of red ink over the next three years.

He sold to Minneapolis banker Carl Pohlad for an amount considerably less than the $50 million the Detroit team brought, or the $32 million that the Cleveland club had sold for about a year later.

After that, Pohlad easily arranged the purchase of the minority shares held by the Tampa group, and that was the end of the Griffith era.

Veeck? He didn't get a nickel out of it, nor ever once see his name in the paper in connection with the proceedings. The man whom other owners had derided for years as a publicity hound had no desire to take credit for a victory he had masterminded. He was content simply to bask in the knowledge that he had evened an old score.

Unbelievably, it took only three years to prove the wisdom of our actions, and today, as I write this, a new era has blossomed. Thanks to the aggressive management of the Pohlad organization, for the first time in the history of the franchise, attendance hit over two million as the Twins achieved what has been dubbed, 'The Impossible Dream.'

October 1987 will always be remembered as the month the Minnesota Twins astounded their loyal and long-suffering fans by winning the American League Pennant to make it to the World Series – and then stunned the nation by winning the series to become the world champions of baseball. At the beginning of the season, Las Vegas book makers set the odds against that happening at 150–1. The phenomenal ascent of the Twins from last place to world champions ignited an explosion of pride, unity, and good will that energized the entire upper Midwest and produced incalculable economic results.

Bill Veeck did more than acquaint me with the weird

17

economics of major-league baseball. He also taught me a lesson that applies in a wide range of business situations.

Most business problems can be solved if you can teach yourself to look beyond the dollar sign. Business revolves around human beings. We're not all in it for the buck. Fight trainer Gil Clancy expresses it, naturally, in sock-in-the-eye fashion. 'The reason I stay in this game after thirty years isn't to get rich. It's to get even.'

It takes all kinds, friends. That's why no one has all the answers. What this book offers is *not* how and what to buy cheap and sell dear. Instead, I'm going to try to help you make money by giving you a better understanding of people.

The first lesson I offer is one of the first I learned when I made my first business deal. I was eleven years old and I'd won a prize for selling the most tickets to the St. Paul Saints opening baseball game. This entrepreneurial coup was scored by telling my friends that if they bought their tickets from me, I could get them into the locker room to meet the ballplayers. It should have been easy. After all, as the Associated Press correspondent in town, my father knew every ballplayer on the team.

Unfortunately, I hadn't bothered to ask him about it beforehand. The day of the game, he was covering a political rally in Minneapolis (in those days, reporters, like doctors, were generalists), and even doing my best 'Jack Mackay's son' number, though I could see the whole team sitting there in their skivvies drinking beer, I couldn't bluff my way past the man at the clubhouse door.

I made it home in one piece, but my credibility with my friends was zero. To top it off, my big prize for selling the most tickets turned out not to be such a big prize after all. It was a season's pass, just the kind of perk my father could have had for the asking.

That introduction to the world of marketing taught me a couple of lessons many adults learn at a much higher cost than I had to pay. *Anyone* can get the order if he's willing to stretch the truth far enough. Whether you tell the truth or not, you *don't* come out a winner just by getting that first big order. The mark of a pro is getting the *reorder*. In the advertising business, they put it a little differently: 'Creative wins 'em; account service loses 'em.' I learned something else that day: The clubhouse men of the world are just waiting for a chance to kick you in the ass. You may not be watching them, but they're watching you, and the more arrogant you are, whether you're an eleven-year-old kid or some self-important business type, the better the odds they'll find a way to get even.

Now you're getting the picture.

What you are going to read about from now on in this book isn't a laundry list of killer closing lines and split-second witticisms that landed the big fish.

It's how the big fish got to be that way and how you can be one, too.

Chapter II

Harvey Mackay's Short Course In Salesmanship

◆

LESSON 1

It's not how much it's worth, it's how much people think it's worth

A speaker is introduced to a roomful of people who have never seen him or heard him before. He begins his presentation by reaching into his pocket, holds up a twenty-dollar bill, and says, 'This twenty is for sale for exactly one dollar. Who wants to buy it?'

Now, be honest. Would you leap to your feet clamoring to get his attention? Or would you wait a few seconds, see what everyone else does, and then after a hand or two goes up, timidly raise your own?

If you're one of the hesitators, you're normal. We've been taught all our lives that only suckers fall for deals like that. But once someone else is willing to take a chance, on no better information than ours, then our greedy little hands pop up, and we tend to go along. The faster others' hands are raised, the greater the demand, and the more likely we are to be part of it. Our sense of what something is worth derives not from the intrinsic value of the object itself – whether it's twenties for a dollar or unusual tulip bulbs or a rare gem – but from the demand that has been created for that object.

Okay, you say, that's Marketing 101. Everyone knows that, but what does it have to do with the real world?

A great deal, it turns out.

I'd like to tell you a story about four of the richest men in North America who absolutely did not understand this very simple concept. A few years from now I feel it will be tucked into the Harvard M.B.A. casebooks along with those other Big Business Boo-boos.

Maybe we can learn something from it.

The scene: the suburbs. The most valuable property in the state (and possibly in the country), fifty acres of prime suburban real estate, becomes available for development when we tear down our old sports stadium and build a new one downtown. Enter: four brothers named Ghermezian – four men from Edmonton, Canada, by way of Iran who became rich first as rug merchants and then as real-estate developers. Their greatest achievement to date is the West Edmonton Mall, the world's largest. This is no ordinary mall: The Ghermezian gimmick involves not only sheer size (hundreds of shops, services, restaurants, etc.) but also a complete entertainment complex, 2½-acre indoor lake, twenty-five ride amusement park, and the lavish $50 million Fantasyland Hotel. The Ghermezians call this mall 'the Eighth Wonder of the World,' and hundreds of thousands of tourists agree with them.

The Ghermezian brothers make a terrific offer. They want to build on the old stadium site a $1.5 billion development that will provide forty thousand new, nonsmokestack jobs at union wages, utilize a vacant piece of land that's not generating a nickle's worth of jobs or taxes, and attract millions of visitors to the state every year.

The governor is delighted with their idea and is ready to

call a special session of the legislature to pass the tax-high-way-improvement-etc. package that will give the Ghermezian proposal a green light.

It sounds like exactly the sort of project every state in the country is dying for. (In fact, a few months before the Ghermezians came on the scene, the state legislature fell over backward and did everything in its power in an unsuccessful bid to attract a new General Motors Saturn automobile plant to the state − a much less attractive facility than the four real-estate moguls were proposing.) There are no catches to the Ghermezian proposal. Their requests for legislative assistance and tax relief are fairly reasonable, they have solid financial backing, and they have a reputation for doing exactly what they propose to do.

Yet in about as much time as it takes to say 'the Amazing Ghermezians,' door after door is slammed in their faces, and the governor quickly backpedals and withdraws his support. It is all the result of a simple mistake in the public-relations approach to the deal: In order to supply something, you must first create a demand.

I could stand on a street corner all day long with twenty-dollar bills for sale at a dollar apiece and only manage to get arrested. Who would believe that anyone would make such a fabulous offer? There must be a catch. If the Ghermezians had done what General Motors did a few months earlier − announce that they would build their facility in the location that offered *them* the best deal − instead of offering *us* such a good deal − we would have fallen all over ourselves to attract them. We wouldn't have to be told why their proposal was attractive. We could tell ourselves because others were competing for it. It's the same old lesson Huck Finn taught Tom Sawyer a hundred years ago. But maybe the tale of the painting of the white picket fence wasn't included in the Ghermezians' child-hood bedtime storybook.

Marketing is not the art of selling. It's not the simple

business of convincing someone to buy. It is the art of creating conditions by which the buyer convinces *himself*. And nothing is more convincing than hard evidence that others want the same thing.

LESSON 2

There are objections to every proposition, no matter how attractive; good salespeople set up situations where the customer sells himself, regardless of the objections

The Japanese have a very simple way of describing the typical American marketing plan: READY? FIRE! AIM.

Apparently that was also the Ghermezian approach. They could have asked themselves a few simple questions: What is it I am selling? How do I create a demand for it? Who am I selling it to and what do they really want? Instead they simply plunged in and began pitching. Let's see what the end result may have been had the Ghermezians done it differently.

Were they selling a mall? No. Jobs and tax revenues? Partly. Bragging rights to something someone else wants? Mostly.

This kind of selling, where the customer must qualify to get the product, is the salesman's dream. And it's the only way you can sell products that have limited intrinsic value but great snob appeal.

You think I'm talking about overpriced imported cars and jewelry? Not really. Those have pretty small price tags when you compare them with some of the really expensive toys, like real-estate developments and major-league franchises. There is no purely economic justification for the huge expenditures made by individuals and cities intent on capturing these crown jewels of conspicuous consumption. What value do you place on ego or uniqueness?

Which is just the kind of situation that GM set up with the Saturn plant.

If you're the Ghermezians, how do you create the same kind of demand?

First, by staying in Edmonton, that mysterious and exotic home of high finance and intrigue, rather than showing up on the first plane. General Motors officials did not travel around the country to sell their proposition. They made announcements from Detroit and stood back while their customers came to them. GM understood the necessity of creating a climate where the customers became their own salesmen, and GM became a kind of referee deciding who would be awarded the sale.

Now, why didn't four shrewd businessmen like the Ghermezians see that when they decided to make their move? Why did they simply blunder onstage waving their twenty-dollar bills in front of a skeptical audience?

For one thing, they thought that if they had the support of the governor, that would be enough.

Wrong.

They forgot to ask two additional questions: Who are my real customers? What is it they really want?

They got part of the answer right: The politicians *were* their ultimate customers. The politicians are the ones who will approve the financing and incentive packages that make such deals work. Once that approval is gained, everything else is simply mechanical: how much to charge per square foot, how many advertising dollars are needed to lure the necessary customers, and so on. But to get to the politicians, you must understand how to motivate them. In their eagerness to get the decision-makers to cast the votes, sign the papers, and smile for the cameras so the business of developing the project could proceed, the Ghermezians lost

25

sight of their customers' real needs. The Ghermezians' customers, the politicians, had customers of their own. The politicians began to get concerned. Were they giving *their* customers, the voters, something they really wanted, something that would make them vote right again at the next election? Here's where the next part of the billion-dollar blunder was made.

LESSON 3

Knowing something about your customer is just as important as knowing everything about your product

Take politicians, for example. A politician will support your proposition only as long as it is politically popular or uncommonly rewarding.

That isn't to say that pols are any less honest or reliable than the rest of us. It's just that politicians must shift positions constantly to keep up with the people they are supposed to be leading. Legislators, particularly in faraway places such as Washington, tend to be a little less reliable than governors, who are under closer local scrutiny, but the same principle holds. It is the duty of someone who wants something from a politician either to (a) create the public climate that makes supporting that position attractive, or (b) do whatever is necessary so that a politico will return a favor from time to time — like fundraising or even organizational work.

Before you choose one tactic or the other, you had better be certain with whom you are dealing. In this case, the governor was the type of politician who thought he had something his constituents would truly want. The Ghermezians and the governor both went public together, and when it became rapidly apparent that the brothers had not created the proper climate of public opinion, the governor backed off.

To the Ghermezians' credit, they finally got the message, hired local lobbyists, and put the pieces back together. After having asked for several *hundred* million dollars at the legislature and getting completely skunked, they got help at the municipal level. The current scaled-down version – call it a mini-mega-mall – might still be the largest development of its kind. But it *could* have been even bigger.

Identifying the customer does not mean that you make your pitch directly to that customer. Selling to the governor in this case was easy . . . too easy. What the Ghermezians should have done was first build a support structure of 'influencers' around that governor – the press, the unions, popular opinion, his own party, and so on – before pitching the main man. That involves a professional PR effort: stories extolling their already successful mall; leaks about competing cities plotting to sweep the Ghermezians into their fold; orchestrated demand for the product from leading opinion-makers. None of this groundwork was laid. Unfortunately (for the Brothers Ghermezian), once the governor discovered he had no crew, it was time to abandon ship.

At Mackay Envelope Corporation, you wouldn't believe how much we know about our customers. The IRS wouldn't believe how much we know about our customers. All our salespeople on our staff fill out a 66-question profile of each one of their customers. We're not talking about the customer's taste in envelopes, either. We want to know, based on observation and routine conversation, what our customer is like as a human being, what he feels strongly about, what he's most proud of having achieved, and what the status symbols are in his office.

When you know your customers, some of their special interests or characteristics, you always have a basis for contacting and talking to them. I have a customer who's a devoted Chicago Cubs baseball fan. That's usually good for at least half a dozen condolence messages a year. I don't sit there scribbling notes about the latest fashions in envelopes. I write about the Cubs; *he* writes about the envelopes.

I have another customer who's a stamp collector. No matter where I go, all over the world, I send him unusual and exotic stamps. I think he must like that. He's been a customer for twenty years, and in all that time, I've met him only once.

Knowing your customer means knowing what your customer really wants. Maybe it is your product, but maybe there's something else, too: recognition, respect, reliability, concern, service, a feeling of self-importance, friendship, help – things all of us care more about as human beings than we care about malls or envelopes.

LESSON 4

The 66-question customer profile

It's critical to know about your customer. We've seen the folly of not having that knowledge. If businesspeople as sophisticated and resource-deep as the Ghermezians can make that mistake, so can we. Armed with the right knowledge, we can outsell, outmanage, outmotivate, and outnegotiate our competitors. Am I overpromising?

Not if you believe, as I do, in the value of information.

All of us gather data about other people – especially people we want to influence. The only question is how well we understand it and what we do with it.

For anyone who feels that this kind of reconnaissance smacks of Big Brotherism, remember the truth about buyers: They came prewired to regard your proposition with suspicion and cynicism. That's their job.

It's your job as a salesperson to neutralize these feelings so your product can get the fair hearing it deserves.

If selling were just a matter of determining who's got the low bid, then the world wouldn't need salespeople. It could all be done on computers. The 'Mackay 66' is designed to convert you from an adversary to a colleague of the people you're dealing with and to help you make sales.

People, not specs, will always be the key in determining who gets the sale. As Lee Iacocca said, 'Anyone who doesn't get along with people doesn't belong in this business, because that's all we've got around here.'

That's exactly why I developed the 66-question customer profile. Yes, what we're talking about here is filling out a form. It does not come as news to me that people don't like to fill out forms, or that salespeople are worse than most that way. Salespeople are Big Picture types, refugees from mathematics, operating strictly from the right/creative side of the brain. I understand that. I accept that. This form is designed with those attitudes in mind.

Collecting this information is easier than you might think. Take the last page, the most important part of the 'Mackay 66.' Customers are remarkably willing to share their management's goals and issues with you. But, salespeople being salespeople, you often just ignore it. The standard attitude is that any piece of paper that isn't a signed order isn't worth reading. I've seen that indifference in the glazed stare of a thousand salespeople, but awareness of the information in the 66 — and knowing how to use it — are what distinguish the pros from the Willy Lomans.

So don't be turned off because I'm offering you a form. It isn't that tough to use. You're probably doing a lot of it already, and the 'Mackay 66' will just help you systematize your information in a way that will make it more useful and accessible.

Though most of the information will come from personal contact with your customer and from observation, you don't have to be the sole collector. Your resources are:

CUSTOMERS	TELEVISION
SUPPLIERS	RECEPTIONISTS
BANKS	SECRETARIES
NEWSPAPERS	ASSISTANTS
TRADE PUBLICATIONS	

And this is the short list.

In our shop, one of the duties of secretaries is to scan the local papers, *The Wall Street Journal*, and *The New York Times* daily. Anything that relates to our top twenty customers is a Must Read for anyone concerned with the account.

The value of the 66 isn't limited to salespeople. As in any business, salespeople leave. The 66 is a way to prevent their accounts from leaving with them. It gets their successor up and running and with a decided timing edge, a much shorter learning curve than would be necessary if the salesperson had to start from scratch.

Because it's all there on paper, the Mackay 66 also helps when salespeople and sales managers are discussing customers.

Two cautionary notes: It's a changing world, so the 66 has to be updated continually; and, because of the kind of private information that often winds up in these questionnaires, they have to be given secure storage, with only numbered copies and no dupes floating around. For the first ten years we used this process, I would take home the files on our top ten accounts every Sunday night and drill the information into my head until I knew it by rote. Although I don't do that anymore, once a year our marketing group and our top operating people sit down and review the material with special emphasis on the final page. This analysis of common customer issues is the launching pad for our planning process.

Now you know *how* it works. The question you're probably asking is, 'Does it work?' Read the 66 now, and then let me try to answer that question.

MACKAY ENVELOPE CORPORATION 66-QUESTION CUSTOMER PROFILE

Date _____

Last updated _____

By _____

Customer

1. Name _____ Nickname _____
   Title _____
2. Company name and address _____
3. Home address _____
4. Telephone: _____
                   Business _____
                   Home _____

5. Birth date and place _____
   Hometown _____
6. Height _____ Weight _____
   _____
   Outstanding physical characteristics _____
   _____
   Examples: balding, great condition, arthritis, severe back problems, etc.)

Education

7. High school and year _____
   College _____
   Graduated when _____ Degrees _____
8. College honors _____ Advanced degrees _____
9. College fraternity or sorority _____
   Sports _____
10. Extracurricular college activities _____
11. If customer didn't attend college, is he/she sensitive about it?
    _____
    What did they do instead? _____
12. Military service _____ Discharge rank _____
    Attitude toward being in the service _____

Family

13. Marital status _____ Spouse's name _____
14. Spouse's education _____

33

15. Spouse's interests/activities/affiliations _____
16. Wedding anniversary _____
17. Children, if any, names and ages _____
_____

    Does client have custody? _____
18. Children's education _____
19. Children's interests (hobbies, problems, etc.) _____
_____

Business Background

20. Previous employment: (most recent first)
    Company _____
    Location _____
    Dates _____ Title _____
    Company _____
    Location _____
    Dates _____ Title _____
21. Previous position at present company: Title _____
    Dates: _____
22. Any 'status' symbols in office? _____
23. Professional or trade associations _____
    Office or honors in them _____
24. Any mentors? _____
25. What business relationship does he/she have with others in
    our company? _____
    _____
26. Is it a good relationship? _____ Why? _____
27. What other people in our company know the customer? ____
    _____
28. Type of connection _____ Nature of relationship _____
    _____
29. What is client's attitude toward his/her company? _____
    _____
30. What is his/her long-range business objective? _____
    _____
31. What is his/her immediate business objective? _____
    _____

34

32. What is of greatest concern to customer at this time: the welfare of the company or his/her own personal welfare? ___

33. Does customer think of the present or the future? _____
Why? _____

Special Interests

34. Clubs or service clubs (Masons, Kiwanis, etc.) _____
_____

35. Politically active? ___ Party ___ Importance to customer ___

36. Active in community? ____ How? _____

37. Religion _____ Active? _____

38. Highly confidential items NOT to be discussed with customer (for example, divorce, member of AA, etc.) _____

39. On what subjects (outside of business) does customer have strong feelings? _____
_____

Lifestyle

40. Medical history (current condition of health) _____

41. Does customer drink? _____ If yes, what and how much? ___

42. If no, offended by others drinking? _____

43. Does customer smoke? _____ If no, object to others? _____

44. Favorite places for lunch _____ Dinner _____

45. Favorite items on menu _____
_____

46. Does customer object to having anyone buy his/her meal? ___

47. Hobbies and recreational interests _____
What does customer like to read? _____
_____

48. Vacation habits _____

49. Spectator-sports interest: sports and teams _____

50. Kind of car(s) _____

51. Conversational interests _____

52. Whom does customer seem anxious to impress? _____
_____

53. How does he/she want to be seen by those people? _____
_____

54. What adjectives would you use to describe customer? _____
_____

55. What is he/she most proud of having achieved? _____
_____

56. What do you feel is customer's long-range personal objective? _____

57. What do you feel is customer's immediate personal goal? ____
_____

The Customer and You

58. What moral or ethical considerations are involved when you work with customer? _____

59. Does customer feel any obligation to you, your company, or your competition? _____ If so, what? _____

60. Does the proposal you plan to make to him/her require customer to change a habit or take an action that is contrary to custom? _____

61. Is he/she primarily concerned about the opinion of others? __

62. Or very self-centered? _____ Highly ethical? _____

63. What are the key problems as customer sees them? _____
_____

64. What are the priorities of the customer's management? _____
_____

Any conflicts between customer and management? _____

65. Can you help with these problems? _____ How? _____

66. Does your competitor have better answers to the above questions than you have? _____

Additional Notes

LESSON 5

The 'Mackay 66' continued: war stories

Flip back to the 66 and look at question 5, 'Birth date and place — Hometown —.' 'So,' You say to yourself, 'Mackay counsels sending customers a birthday card? Big deal.' Wait a minute. Sure, the customer gets a birthday card. But there's more. Remember as kids we had an intuition never to ask for something if our folks were in a terrible mood. But when we sensed they were content, we'd hit them up for whatever the market would bear. Timing's everything, isn't it? At our company, we have our customers' birthdays on computer, and they get a birthday card, of course. But guess what? That buyer also gets called on in person – and asked out to lunch – when that special day of the year rolls around.

It's not too surprising occasionally to see our sales break the sound barrier on the same day our customer is celebrating a birthday. As for the hometown of the buyer – it's the source of an endless supply of news clips to mail in. And you don't even have to clip them yourself. If it's worth it to you, subscribe to a clipping service – or pick up that hometown paper occasionally. To be armed with knowledge about Hometown, U.S.A., gives you a subject customers can talk about eight days a week.

'Education.' Questions 7–12. One day I called on a

buyer who, it turned out, had graduated from the same high school I did – about fifteen years earlier. We both had the fabled Miss Malmon for English. The yarns we told were fabulous; the envelopes he bought were even more fabulous. I figured it out the other day. This buyer has purchased over 150 million envelopes from me. I wonder why.

'Family.' Questions 13–19. I luckily overheard a buyer's secretary on the phone arranging to have her twelve-year-old daughter driven to her gymnastics event. Obviously, I asked about the daughter. Suddenly there I was, watching the Mighty Mite compete in the parallel bars event. A month later, after having brought myself up to speed in gymnastics, I mentioned it to the buyer – and got my first order the same day.

'Business background.' Question 22. 'Any "status" symbols in the office?' is a good question to key on. I called on a *Fortune* 500 company in New York – having learned that the most important reading a salesperson can do is to read the wall of his prospect's office while waiting for him to get off the phone – and noticed a picture of the company president awarding the buyer a certificate for writing a position paper on unemployment. A week later I sent him a book on unemployment. The orders have never stopped coming.

'Lifestyle.' Questions 40–57. Tickets to the game are always a good ice-breaker, particularly if you go with the customer. And don't take it for granted we're just talking about men here.

I'd been calling on a purchasing agent in Chicago for three years without her ever once even asking me to quote a job.

I found out she was a wrestling fan.

Overnight I became a wrestling fan. I popped into her office, told her I had great contacts for ringside tickets to – yes, this was many years ago – Gorgeous George and would she care to go or have me make the tickets available so she could go with someone else?

It was a real struggle for her to accept. She wasn't naïve,

she knew I was trying to capture her business, but the lure of ringside seats was too much to resist. Though she decided to accept, she insisted on paying for the tickets.

Three years of hard work with no results — and to be truthful, it took another year before she even asked me to bid a job — and two more before we got an order. Six years. But it was the 66 that did it, and the business we've done since then made it worth the wait.

The payoff: The proof is in the envelope. Not the Mackay envelope. The pay envelope. Mackay Envelope's salespeople earn more than double our industry's national average. There's just one reason: the Mackay 66.

Once you attach your personality to a proposition, people start reacting to the personality and stop reacting to the proposition

LESSON 7

Racial and religious prejudice and human envy have not been eliminated as of the date of publication of this book

Most sales manuals will tell you that the most important thing you are selling is yourself. This book won't. In my opinion, selling yourself can sometimes be a very bad idea . . . because very often, my friend, you and I are lousy products.

Our challenge, whether we are salespeople or negotiators or managers or entrepreneurs is to make others see the advantage to themselves in responding to our proposal. Understanding our subjects' personalities is vital. Let them shine. Our own personalities are subordinate.

High profiles fit most businessmen like a cheap suit. Yes, I know Lee Iacocca is no shrinking violet. And he seems to be doing all right. You're not Lee Iacocca, and neither am I, and neither are the Ghermezian brothers. General Motors got state legislators across the country to do somersaults for their Saturn proposal, in part because the company managed to hide behind its corporate identity throughout the entire process. There were no individuals with strange-sounding names or funny accents or huge personal wealth for the press to take potshots at. Just a large, well-known, amorphous company. Who are those people? No one really knew, and they stood a better chance of getting what they wanted that way.

In the 'good old days,' salesmen were matched to the ethnic makeup of their clientele. You sent your Irish salesman out to call on Irish customers; Jewish salesmen, Jewish customers, and so on. That's changed a bit. As some minorities have become more secure, shrewd sales managers recognize that customers who formerly were serviced along strict ethnic lines want to signal their group's acceptance into the mainstream by dealing with people who do not reflect their own backgrounds. Okay, those people get serviced by not-whatever-the-customer-happens-to-be types. But each case is different. That's why at my company we put a lot of thought into analyzing our customers before we decide where to place that account.

If you aren't sure of your customers, stay home and hire someone who knows the territory. Sometimes you'll find that your prospects are more comfortable and receptive around people whose styles are local. For instance, people from the prestige cities like New York and San Francisco tend to feel that no one knows as much about anything as they do. After all, if we had any talent that's where we'd be living, wouldn't we? Why should they listen to someone from Peoria? On the other hand, those of us from lesser cities often tend to be in awe of the out-of-town expert, the definition of an expert still being anyone from more than fifty miles away. In those cases you have to be prepared to dazzle by tossing the properly elegant and aloof three-piece-suiters into the mix.

There's a correct approach for your sales situation, whether it's hiring the right spokesperson, operating behind the corporate veil, or creating demand for your proposition. The key is knowing your customer, not just marching in and offering an objectively attractive deal.

LESSON 8

How to handle the tough prospect

Now that you know what can go wrong, and some of what you need to know to make it right, it's time you learned some of the ways you can use the information you've won.

My definition of a salesperson is not someone who can get the order. Anyone can get the order if he tells enough lies – for example, about price or delivery time.

A great salesperson is someone who can get the order – and the reorder – from a prospect who is already doing business with someone else.

It all starts out with the sales call. I have never made a cold call in my life. Before I see anyone on a sales call for the first time, I see to it that I'm introduced. The salesperson's classic dilemma is set out in an ad done forty years ago by McGraw-Hill to promote – what else – advertising. It pictures a green-eyeshade, rolltop-desk-type curmudgeon facing the reader, who is cast in the role of the salesman. The Tough Prospect says:

- I don't know who you are.
- I don't know your company.
- I don't know what your company stands for.
- I don't know your company's customers.
- I don't know your company's products.
- I don't know your company's reputation.
- Now – what was it you wanted to sell me?

If you're selling for a big outfit, an IBM, your introduction is made, in part, by the company's advertising, marketing, and public-relations program. IBM's solid reputation is a powerful silent salesperson that accompanies every sales call.

If you're not selling for an IBM, you need another effective entry. The best is a recommendation from one of your own customers, someone already known to your prospect.

Like most salespeople, I've spent a lifetime trying to build a network of customers and friends who will give me a line of communication into almost every office in my city.

There are two ways to do it: retail and wholesale. Retail means the one-at-a-time kind of contacts that are built up through participation in community or social activities. Wholesale means the recognition, and acceptance, extended by people who don't know you personally but who have heard about you as a speaker, read your articles, or read about your civic activities in the papers.

Either method can help break down the classic barriers to a cold call.

When I don't have a personal entry, there are other tactics I fall back on. If your company is publicly held, take a look at your annual report. Most such reports are designed to be sales tools, the targets being the company's stockholders and stockbrokers. No reason that target can't be enlarged to include the company's customers. I've bought one share of stock in almost all the publicly held companies in our area. It drives my broker nuts, but I always tell him that every one of these one-share orders we can convert into a customer, I'll give him a hundred-share order in the stock. We keep the annual reports in a library in our office where our salespeople can get at them. Some do. There are annual reports there that are almost as dog-eared as barber shop copies of *Playboy*.

If your company doesn't lend itself to the annual-report game, maybe the prospect's company does. Find out as much information as you can about that company, from either public sources, like your broker, or the city library's business section or from private sources, like Dun & Bradstreet, or your banker, lawyer, or accountant. (You say they aren't supposed to disclose this kind of information? Well, if you're talking about *their* clients, they aren't, but it's all right if they're talking about someone else's.) You can even check prospects out through other, noncompetitive suppliers.

Somewhere within six blocks of every company is a favored watering hole. I know of one salesman who has developed the technique of waiting in his car across from the prospect's parking lot on Friday afternoons for the five-o'clock whistle and then following the procession to the saloon of choice. Whatever it is he wants to know, whether it's about a prospect or a competitor, can usually be uncorked in this convivial atmosphere. He says he has perfected the ability to lose convincingly in every bar sport in America: pool/shuffleboard/pinball/ 'and I'm still working on darts.'

Armed with either your annual report, your prospect's, or both, you are now in a position to write the Tough Prospect, tell him how good your outfit is, read him back enough about his own to demonstrate you've done your homework, and ask for an appointment.

Naturally, the whole heap ends up in the round file. You're not done yet. You're about to call to make an appointment to see the Tough Prospect. Your call is answered by the company receptionist. You do *not* ask for Mr T.P. You say, 'I'm going to ask you *in a moment* to connect me with Mr T.P.'s office, but before I do, could you kindly remind me of the name of his secretary?' She will. *Then* ask her to connect you with Mr T.P.'s office.

'Hello. Angela? I'm Harvey Mackay, President of Mackay Envelope Corporation. [Straight to her brain. Who is this guy? How does he know my name? Have I met him?] I've written Mr T.P. within the past two weeks, and now I'm calling him from Minneapolis. I would like to see Mr T.P. I would like to see him for exactly three hundred seconds. I will go as far as Guam or Sri Lanka just for the purpose of seeing him for those three hundred seconds, and if I take any longer, I'll donate five hundred dollars to T.P.'s favourite charity . . . which I believe is the Boy Scouts, isn't it?'

When you've done your homework, when you've looked up your prospect in *Who's Who*, and done some reconnaissance with his suppliers, then you know you're right. And what an impression it makes.

The proposition is intriguing enough so that it generally works. Will this hard-charger actually get in and out in five minutes?

The truth is, I never take the full five minutes. I simply introduce myself and say, 'As you may know, we're bidding on your contract. I just came here to tell you, as president of Mackay Envelope, that we regard your business as significant. If we are fortunate enough to receive your business, I'll take a personal interest in seeing to it that you will receive the service and craftsmanship you have every right to expect.' That's it.

In and out in two and one half minutes. And I follow up with a presigned letter postmarked that day from Minneapolis thanking him for his time and restating the same pitch I gave him in person . . . and if it seems appropriate, a *receipt* for a check for $100 to his favorite charity. 'I just wanted you to know I promised Angela I'd send a check for $500 to your favorite charity if I wasn't out of your office in five minutes. Even though I made the deadline, I've always been an admirer of the Boy Scouts and have sent them a small donation.'

Does it always work? No. Does anything?

But it works better than anything else I've tried. One final wrinkle. If 'Angela' won't make the appointment for you, try to get T.P. to call back by saying, 'Angela, even if he won't see me, perhaps he will talk to me. I am going to be in my office at the following times: two P.M. to three P.M. today; eight A.M. to noon tomorrow.' And so on. Then instruct your secretary as follows: 'When and if Mr T.P. calls at any of these times, you're to say, "Oh, yes, Mr T.P., he's been expecting your call. I'll put you right through!"'

You don't have to confine that device to T.P.'s. Anyone you're playing telephone tag with will appreciate knowing *when* he can reach you, so leave the times as part of your message, and make sure your secretary is in on it, so she can make a fuss over the caller and call him by name (' . . . I'll put you right through!') when he does call back.

All right, you've done all that, you've talked to T.P., you've sent him little love notes for two years, mailed him a million boxes of apricots from The Fruit of the Month Club, and you *still* haven't gotten even a whiff of an order. So what? Be patient, you will. You have positioned yourself in the best possible spot you can be in: Number Two, and a very strong Number Two, because no one, including Number One, is going to half the trouble you are to keep this account aware of your interest.

Politicians know that being a front runner like a Hart or a Muskie can be a very vulnerable position. If the front runner stumbles, it is Number Two who is there to pick up the votes.

You've got something else going for you, too. Consider for a moment the Law of Large Numbers. An entire industry, insurance, has been built on that one principle. There are 240 million living Americans. The Insurance people can tell you within one-fourth of one percent just how many of us are going to die within the next twelve months – and how – and where – and in what age bracket, sex, color, and creed. That's pretty amazing. The only thing they can't tell us is *who*.

Apply the Law of Large Numbers to your prospect list. Position yourself as Number Two to every prospect on your list, and keep adding to that list. I can promise you that if your list is long enough, there are going to be Number Ones that retire or die or lose their territories for a hundred other reasons and succumb to the Law of Large Numbers. What I can't tell you is *which one*. But fortunately, as in the insurance business, 'which one' doesn't matter. All that matters is that you have the perseverance and patience to position yourself as Number Two to enough different people, and the Law of Large Numbers will do for you what it has done for the insurance industry: You will be an extremely successful and wealthy salesperson. If you're standing second in line, in enough lines, sooner or later you're going to move up to Number One, and the amazing thing is that no one else *ever* uses this strategy. It works not just in business but in your personal life as well.

LESSON 9

Create your own private club

Country clubs and business clubs, with selective membership and their own dining and athletic facilities, exist for one reason: to create an atmosphere that makes it easier to do business (and survive for one other: the tax laws). Let's say you're entertaining customers in a town where you don't belong to a club. How do you give yourself the patina of respectability a club imparts and create that cozy, club-like atmosphere in a place where nobody knows you?

Easy.

The best way, of course, is to get someone you know in town to let you use their club and sign a tab in the member's name. That's a whale of an imposition, but if you have a friend willing to let you do it, do it.

If not, pick the best restaurant in town. You, not your secretary, should call beforehand, ask for the *maître d'* and say you're from out of town, you're entertaining one of your top customers, and 'You won't be sorry when I get there.' Describe yourself and say you would like to be greeted by name. Tell him you want a table that has three characteristics: not near a swinging kitchen door, not near a busing station, and not in a high-traffic entrance area. Let him know you would like their best waiter. No menu. Just a recital of the choicest three or four items being served that day. Give the *maître d'* your credit card number. Tell him to add 20 percent to the bill for the waiter, but not to present the bill at the table. Give your office phone number for verification, or if you have to, stop by in advance and sign the bill.

At the end of your meal, watch carefully for the startled expression on your customer's face when you utter the magic words 'Let's go' and leave him wondering when you signed the check.

By doing a little advance planning you've achieved two major objectives: you've avoided an awkward moment for your customer by not signing or paying in cash, and you've just made the best restaurant in town your own private club.

LESSON 10

Short notes yield long results

Do you always buy a car from the same salesperson? Your shoes? Any tangible item? Of course not.

A new car costs more than $10,000 these days; it's a major purchase decision for anyone. I buy one every couple of years, but I have never once heard from any car salesperson – or any salesperson of any substantial item – once I'd made the purchase from him. No thank-you note. No 'We just got a new shipment in.' No nothing.

Yet many of the successful people I know are constantly sending out short notes. Lou Holtz, the Notre Dame football coach; Pat Fallon, the chairman of the country's hottest advertising agency; Wheelock Whitney, who built one of the nation's most successful brokerage firms. They're all masters of the short note. 'I want you to know how much I enjoyed our meeting/your gift/your hospitality/whatever'; 'Congratulations on your new financing/house/plant/wife/kid's performance at tennis/whatever'; 'Here's an item about envelopes/gold/tennis/marketing seminars/whatever I thought you might be interested in.'

They're hand-written, hand-stamped, and mailed the same day the item appears or is announced or we've had a meeting. It takes only a moment. It's all a matter of personal recognition and courtesy, as it is to remember names and take a personal interest in the people with whom you work. It's a major part of the reason why Holtz,

Fallon, and Whitney are successful – and why I've never bought a car from the same person twice.

Keep this habit in mind even if you're only on the first or second step of the ladder. A young woman I know, fresh out of Brown University and hot to break into advertising, had about as much chance connecting with a job on Mad Ave as a young actress has of landing a part four blocks east of Madison on Broadway. She struggled through the usual months of rejection and alarming dependence on the medications of Dr. Scholl. Finally, an interview seemed to go well on both sides of the desk. That had happened before and she knew she was a long way from having the job sewn up. She went back to her apartment, composed and typed a creative letter of appreciation, and hand-delivered it that same day to the maybe-boss-to-be. End of story? She got the job – against tough competition – and later learned it was the letter that did the trick.

LESSON 11

The second-best place to look for new business

Every business book will tell you about the 80/20 rule: 80 percent of your business comes from 20 percent of your customers.

Every business book also will tell you to work that customer list for more business and more prospects.

It's good advice.

But what about the flip side of that equation? If 20 percent of your customers are 80 percent of your business, then, when you're the customer and not the salesman, you're also 80 percent of the business to 20 percent of your own suppliers.

Look at your supplier list. Shouldn't these people, who are dependent upon you for their livelihoods, be a major source of both business and prospects?

My suppliers have to get their envelopes from someone. That someone is me.

...

LESSON 12

What every salesperson – and not enough entrepreneurs – know

Ask a roomful of entrepreneurs what the sweetest sound in the world is and they lean toward the crisp crinkle of freshly minted currency or the dull thud of a competitor's body hitting the pavement.

Ask anyone in the sales game and they'll tell you that it's the sound of their name on someone else's lips.

I know the headmaster of a private school who makes it a practice to learn the names of each of the over one thousand kids attending his school. If they're new and he hasn't met them, he learns their names by studying their pictures. On the first day of each year, when the buses arrive to drop off the kids at school, he greets each one by name as they get off the bus. Imagine how reassuring it is to a frightened first-grader, suddenly thrust into strange surroundings, to be recognized immediately by an adult who is in charge of his life. Or to the child's anxious parents who have plunked down $5,000 for tuition. When they ask Junior how it went the first day, they discover that the headmaster of the school has taken a personal interest in their child.

In the twelve years that headmaster has been at the school, enrollment has more than doubled, the school has moved to a grand new facility that is clearly the finest in the area, and the endowment has been increased sixfold. Not all the result of learning those names, of course, but it certainly didn't hurt to have a headmaster who understood that his performance as a salesperson was as important as his role as an educator.

LESSON 13

Keep your eye on your time, not on your watch

Knowing what to do isn't enough if you haven't developed the self-discipline to do it. The headmaster who learned to recognize his one thousand students had no extraordinary gifts of memory. He learned it the same way he learned Latin when he was a high school freshman when he locked himself in his room every evening for a week and spent the time drilling himself with handmade flash cards. Instead of '*Amo, amas, amat*' on one side and 'I love, you love, he loves' on the other, there were his students' pictures on the front and their names on the back.

Most of us quit doing that sort of thing in ninth grade. He didn't.

It amazes me that so many salespeople are seized by inertia and act as if they can continue to cling to their jobs without having to exert themselves.

I have known successful salespeople who were drunks, gamblers, liars, thieves ... but I have never known a successful salesperson who sat on his ass all day.

With all the Anonymous groups we have for dealing with human weakness, why is it we haven't organized to combat the most dangerous, expensive, and self-destructive habit of all: wasting time? You can do all those other nasty things and still make a decent living. But if you blow off your nine to fives on useless, time-consuming behavior, you will *fail*.

A salesperson really has nothing to sell but his time. His product exists independently of anything he adds to it; his personality will win him or lose him accounts initially, but if he isn't around to provide service and be accessible to his customers, he'll lose those accounts.

The mark of a good salesperson is that his customer doesn't regard him as a salesperson at all, but a trusted and indispensable adviser, an auxilliary employee who, fortunately, is on someone else's payroll.

It takes energy and self-discipline to sell. Your customer doesn't care if you make the call. *You*, the salesperson, have to care. Despite all the psychological gimmicks designed to motivate salespeople to make calls, like bullpens, sales contests, sales meetings, and motivational training, salespeople still contrive to find 1,001 ways to avoid investing the one asset they have that will invariably bring results: their time.

Why?

I wish I knew.

But I do know that a salesperson doesn't have to be a Lee Iacocca or an Elizabeth Dole to be successful. Just follow one simple rule: Set up a schedule with a fixed number of calls to be made every working day, and complete that schedule. If you make ten stops but only one eyeball-to-eyeball sales call, you've made only one call.

As a salesperson, keeping track of your time is the moral equivalent of a dieter counting calories, except you are monitoring your output, not your intake.

It is an absolutely fail-safe method – the only one there is – to ensure success. If you give yourself a reasonable work program and follow it, you'll hit the top of the charts. It's my experience that salespeople who do monitor themselves this way actually give themselves a tougher program to follow than their sales managers give them. That's because we know ourselves well enough to know that our real capacity far exceeds the average expectations others have for us.

LESSON 14

If you don't have a destination, you'll never get there

Setting goals is simply the long-term version of keeping track of your time. Actually, a three-step process is involved:

- Setting goals
- Developing a plan to achieve those goals
- Keeping track of your time to make sure your plan gets executed

When I was in Japan in 1983, we had a series of seminars in which we heard speeches from the leaders of Japan's largest industrial concerns. We heard from the top officers of Honda, Sony, Mitsubishi, and the head of the biggest enterprise of all, the eighty-eight-year-old president of Matsushita Electric.

Persuading them to speak to us was quite a coup, because the Japanese system is much more rigidly structured than ours, and they regard appearing before the troops in this fashion as somewhat beneath their dignity.

And if giving speeches was regarded as a crude Occidental custom, imagine how they felt about answering questions.

But when our eighty-eight-year-old headliner addressed us, he spoke eloquently and profoundly. Then came the questions:

Question: 'Mr President, does your company have long-range goals?'

Answer: 'Yes.'

Question: 'How long are your long-range goals?'

Answer: 'Two hundred fifty years.'

Question: 'What do you need to carry them out?'

Answer: 'Patience.'

Sounds like a joke. But if it's so funny, how come every time we compete with them, they bury us? Everybody and every business needs a set of basic goals and beliefs, but most of us are seat-of-the-pants, one-day-at-a-time operators. Our goals are fuzzy and our plans for achieving them non-existent.

IBM's basic plan for achieving the company's goals consists of three simple parts: respect for the individual, whether it's a customer, employee, or supplier; pursuit of excellence; and outstanding customer service.

Goals don't have to be elaborate, either, just realistic. IBM has four basic goals: to grow at least as fast as the computer industry itself; to become the industry's lowest-cost producer; to offer the best technology; and to sustain high profits.

Nothing fancy there.

Your personal plans and goals don't even have to be that complicated.

How about a goal like improving your sales ranking one quartile, or adding X more accounts, Y more income, Z more total sales? If that kind of basic planning and goal-setting has helped make IBM the IBM of business, shouldn't you be doing it, too?

One of my good friends gave me her definition of a goal, and it's the best one I've ever heard. 'A goal is a dream with a deadline.' Write yours down — because that's the only way you'll give them the substance they need to force you to carry them out.

59

LESSON 15

Believe in yourself, even when no one else does

Remember the four-minute mile? People had been trying to achieve it since the days of the ancient Greeks. In fact, folklore has it that the Greeks had lions chase the runners, thinking that would make them run faster. They also tried tigers' milk — not the stuff you get down at the health-food store, but the real thing. Nothing worked. So they decided it was impossible. And for thousands of years everyone believed it. It was physiologically impossible for a human being to run a mile in four minutes. Our bone structure was all wrong. Wind resistance too great. Inadequate lung power. There were a million reasons.

Then one man, one single human being, proved that the doctors, the trainers, the athletes, and the millions and millions before him who tried and failed, were all wrong. And miracle of miracles, the year *after* Roger Bannister broke the four-minute mile, thirty-seven other runners broke the four-minute mile, and the year after that three hundred runners broke the four-minute mile.

A few years ago, in New York, I stood at the finish line of the Fifth Avenue Mile and watched thirteen out of thirteen runners break the four-minute mile in a single race. In other words, the runner who finished dead last would have been regarded as having accomplished the impossible a few decades ago.

What happened? There were no great breakthroughs in training. Human bone structure didn't suddenly improve. But human attitudes did.

Think about the stonecutter: He hammers at his rock a hundred times without denting it. On the hundred-and-first blow, the rock will split in two. You know it is not that blow that did it but all that had gone before. You *can* accomplish your goals . . . if you set them. Who says you're not tougher, smarter, better, harder-working, more able than your competition? It doesn't matter if *they* say you can't do it. What matters, the only thing that matters, is if *you* say it. Until Bannister came along, we all believed in the experts. Bannister believed in himself . . . and changed the world. If you believe in yourself, well, then, there's nothing you can't accomplish. So don't quit. Don't ever quit.

LESSON 16

Seek role models

Well, the truth is, we're not all Bannisters . . . and we don't have to be first to succeed. As one famous political figure said, 'It's the pioneers who get all the arrows.'

In the restaurant business, you never want to be the first operator in a location. Usually the place has to pass through three or four sets of hands before there's a fit between the restaurant, the location, and the market that's being served.

The trick is to benefit from the Bannisters without having to take the arrows. The people who ran the four-minute mile *after* Bannister had done it succeeded in large part because they had Bannister as a role model to prove it could be done.

When Bannister accomplished it, the others were able to psych themselves up and do the same thing. Who (or what) is psyching *you* up? If you think about why you are the way you are, chances are it has a lot to do with trying to be like someone you admired. You observed and you copied that person's mannerisms. Sometimes, to win his or her approval, you patterned your whole lifestyle after that person. And you didn't become permanently cynical just because you discovered at age fourteen that Mom and Dad weren't perfect and that Simon and Garfunkel were right: Joe DiMaggio *has* gone and he ain't ever coming back.

You never stop needing role models. The Bannisters and

the superstars in every other field keep right on holding role models in front of their eyes long after they've become role models themselves. They study them, copy them, compete with them, and even try to surpass them. It doesn't end with childhood. They're constantly goading themselves to meet new challenges. They top old role models, then they find new ones. They top themselves, and they set new goals. What better way to measure yourself, to feel good about yourself, and to achieve than trying to be like people whom you admire? Look at yourself in the mirror. If you *like* what you see, don't forget that you want to feel the same way tomorrow morning and the morning after.

LESSON 17

Fantasize

When you've lived in a city like New York, you take your major-league status for granted. But when it's the Minneapple and not the Big Apple, being in the majors takes on cosmic significance. Lose those teams and you've lost your civic identity. Ten years ago, before the Calvin Crisis I described earlier, Minneapolis and St. Paul had their first scare about losing their major-league sports franchises, the Minnesota Twins and the Minnesota Vikings.

The problem was our stadium; it was the standard outdoor variety and for our area hopelessly outdated. Upgrading the stadium wasn't the answer. With Minnesota's long winters, any outdoor facility, no matter how modern, is virtually unusable during the last half of the football season and the first few weeks of baseball.

If we were going to keep the teams, we were told we needed a new stadium.

I'd been a sports nut all my life. I didn't want to go back to sitting on a wooden bench rooting for a Park Board softball team. I didn't have the resources to indulge in the ultimate fantasy of buying a team.

So I went to work to try to save our teams by becoming active in the civic program to build a new $75 million stadium, and ultimately I became chairman of the stadium task force. When I started, I thought it would take one year. It took seven. Seven hard, uncertain, frustrating years.

Years when most of the time nothing seemed to go right. From the time I got started until the Hubert H. Humphrey Metrodome was built, I had a fantasy. I would be the one to throw out the first ball. Not the mayor, not the governor, not Joe DiMaggio, but me. I saw it in my mind's eye a thousand times. And, of course, I finally did it.

That's what I did when I was thirteen and dreamed of owning a factory. That's what I did when I owned the factory and dreamed of selling the largest and most prestigious account in town and finally achieved it. In fact, for five years, during the era when men actually wore hats, I had the words 'General Mills' pasted inside the crown of my hat so I saw it every time I put my hat on. An absolutely unavoidable way to remind myself of what I had to do.

I came to realize that fantasizing, projecting yourself into successful situations, is one of the most powerful means there is to achieve personal goals.

It's what an athlete does when he comes onto the field to kick a field goal with three seconds on the clock, sixty thousand people in the stands, thirty million watching on TV, and the game in the balance.

As the kicker begins his move, he automatically makes the hundred tiny adjustments necessary to achieve the mental picture he has formed in his mind so many times . . . since he was a kid . . . the picture of himself kicking the winning field goal. Great athletes seem to have something in common: the ability to *project*. Even in the middle of the action, they see things happen a split second before they happen.

Human survival itself very often depends on a kind of future vision, seeing oneself in specific situations as a healthy, thriving, creative person.

There was a study done of concentration camp survivors. What were the common characteristics of those who did not succumb to disease and starvation in the camp? I met a man named Victor Frankl who was a living answer to that question. He was a successful Viennese psychiatrist before the Nazis threw him into such a camp. 'There is only one reason,' he said in a speech, 'why I am here today. What kept me alive was you. Others gave up hope. I dreamed. I dreamed that someday I would be here, telling you how I, Victor Frankl, had survived the Nazi concentration camps. I've never been here before, I've never seen any of you before, I've never given this speech before. But in my dreams, in my dreams, I have stood before you and said these words a thousand times.'

Dream on.

LESSON 18

The easiest, least expensive, and most neglected form of advertising

Did you ever notice how many people happen to work in office buildings more than one story in height?

And how many of these same people happen to look out the window from time to time?

Paint your company name and/or logo on the top of your trucks. It costs practically nothing. Advertisers spend sums that would dazzle even a TV evangelist to capture a sliver of a major urban market. In a world where advertisers spend a fortune just to be on the back of ticket envelopes, the painless gimmick of painting the top of your trucks is ignored. We've been doing it for twenty-five years, and we're known locally as, you guessed it, 'the company that paints its name on the top of its trucks.' What I've never been able to figure out is why everyone else doesn't do it.

Paint your wagon.

LESSON 19

Show me a guy who thinks he's a self-made man and I'll show you the easiest sell in the world

All you have to do is make him think it's his idea.

Chapter III

HARVEY MACKAY'S SHORT COURSE ON NEGOTIATION

◆

LESSON 20

Smile and say no until your tongue bleeds

No. No. No. No. No. No. No. No. No. No. No. No. No. No. No.
No. No. No. No. No. No. No. No. No. No. No. No. No. No. No.
No. No. No. No. No. No. No. No. No. No. No. No. No. No. No.
No. No. No. No. No. No. No. No. No . . .

Maybe tomorrow. You'll be amazed how the terms of your deals will improve when you learn to say NO. There were one hundred bank failures in the United States in 1986. How many do you think were caused because the bankers said NO to too many terrific loans?

As a buyer, you have to be aware that the seller is constantly measuring you, and moving in for the kill. Time is almost always the seller's enemy, not yours. The longer you take, the longer you have the use of your own money and control over the terms of any deal, and the more likely those terms are to improve. That's why sellers always couch their deals in terms of buy *now*. If you don't, they're going to have to give you a better deal. And what seller wants to do that?

While the seller is trying to set you up with the 'Who is my customer and what does he really want' bit, you should be aware of it and take appropriate countermeasures.

Years ago, long before the days of professional agents, I acted as an unpaid agent for a great Big 10 football player – let's call him I. C. Anderson, or 'Iceman,' or 'Intensive Care.' They all pretty much describe his speciality: providing orthopedic surgeons with an outstanding assortment of professional challenges. He had been drafted in the first round by both the Toronto Argonauts of the Canadian Football League and the Baltimore Colts of the NFL. I.C. was one of nine children, a poor black kid who had rarely seen a nickel in his life. Obviously I wanted to strike the best deal I could for him and tried to get a bidding war going between the two rival owners, John Bassett of Toronto and Carroll Rosenbloom, then of Baltimore. Bassett had made his fortune as owner of a Toronto newspaper. Rosenbloom made his pile in the rag business and sports. They were similar in six ways. They were both rich, competitive, and hard-nosed. Extremely rich, extremely competitive, and extremely hard-nosed. I was way out of my league.

I let Rosenbloom know we were first going to Toronto. We met with Bassett, and he made I.C. a very attractive offer. At that point, every instinct, every cell in my body told me to get out of Bassett's office and on to Baltimore. 'Thank you, Mr Bassett. We'll certainly consider your generous offer, and we'll let you know,' I said.

Bassett gave me a teeny-weeny smile. 'Just one other thing,' said Bassett. 'My proposal is good only for as long as you are in this room. The instant you leave, I'm calling Mr Rosenbloom in Baltimore and telling him that I have no further interest in your man's services.'

After standing there with my pants down around my ankles for the next minute or two, I asked him if it would be all right 'if I could confer with my client in the next room.' Permission granted.

'I.C.,' I said, taking him to the window and whispering to cross up the mikes I was sure were hidden in the table in the middle of the room, 'we've got to buy some time and get to Baltimore immediately. Pretend you're having a mental breakdown and can't deal with the pressure. Or maybe I'll tell him I have to get back to Minneapolis for labor negotiations.'

I.C. looked at me as if I were the one having the mental breakdown. All that money, and here I was playing games with his future. An All-American he was; Laurence Olivier he wasn't. We decided to go with the labor negotiations bit.

'Mr Bassett, I really do have to get back to Minneapolis tonight for labor negotiations. I have a lot on my mind. I'll let you know tomorrow.'

Bassett reached for the phone. Was he calling Rosenbloom? No, his own secretary. 'Are any of our three Learjets around? I want one to take Mr Mackay and I.C. back to Minneapolis.' Three Learjets. I.C. panting over my shoulder. My pants were down around my ankles again. I had been caught in a bald-faced lie. There seemed to be only one thing left to do.

'Mr Bassett, I'm going to save you the trouble of making that phone call to Baltimore. We're turning down your offer,' I said.

I.C. thought I was crazy, of course, and I even thought I was crazy. But it worked. We went to Baltimore the next day and signed with Carroll Rosenbloom for a better deal than the one Bassett had offered. I.C. played ten years for Baltimore and starred in two Super Bowls, and when Carroll Rosenbloom traded his Baltimore franchise for the Los Angeles Rams, he took only one player with him out to California: I.C. Anderson.

I had learned the two most important lessons any negotiator can learn. First, be prepared to say NO. *No one* ever went broke because he said NO too often. Second, the most powerful tool in any negotiation is information.

71

Bassett's scenario was designed to get Anderson to sign before he left that room for only one reason: He had a hell of a lot better idea of what Rosenbloom was willing to offer than I had. I was lucky. My instincts told me to get out of there without signing. It worked that time, but in the long run, instincts are no match for information.

LESSON 21

Send in the clones

Say you want to buy a house, or a business . . . a big-ticket, one-of-a-kind item.

Nothing's tougher than finding out what the seller's *real* price is.

There's a way.

You clone yourself. You hire a substitute, a ringer.

There's a man who actually makes a living doing this in L.A., and there probably are many more across the country. If you can't find one, create one. A lawyer or an accountant will do nicely.

Let's say we're talking about a house. The ringer meets the seller and asks the price. The seller says $189,000. The buyer reaches into his pocket, pulls out his checkbook, and begins to write out a check, a low-ball check.

'I'm prepared to write you a check right now for $145,000.'

At this point we begin to get the true price. The seller reacts either by getting offended and refusing to deal, or by trying to keep the deal alive. Since people selling their own homes sometimes think they're parting with the crown jewels, if your clone accomplishes nothing else, he's spared you from being blown out of the water before you even get a toe wet.

If the seller is irate and won't deal, we know that his price is, for the time being, $189,000.

73

But seven times out of ten, your seller, probably seeing a real live buyer in front of him for the first time in ages, begins to take him very seriously and starts to negotiate. He may counter on the spot. Let's say $175,000. In which case, you now have a much better idea of what he's really willing to take. Or he may stall. Regardless, if there's *any* glimmer of hesitation, you now know more about his price than he knows about yours . . . before he's ever met you. You may have begun to tap into the mother lode of all negotiating tools: information.

The next step is to wait a week, then send in another ringer, with a slightly different line. He may offer a higher price and be impossible on terms, or he may even try a slightly lower price. I'll pay much more if you'll let *me* name the terms.

He'll pick up more information. And he'll help drill a lower price into the seller's skull as the level at which buyers are willing to deal.

If you still want to step in, you not only have a good idea what the real price is, you not only have conditioned the seller to expect a lower-than-advertised price, you have also arrived at this happy state of affairs without yourself having antagonized the seller with a low-ball offer.

It sure worked for me when I was trying to buy out my biggest competitor. By the time I came into the picture, I not only had an excellent idea of the original price, but also all their figures, accounts, records, the works. It doesn't always work, of course, but if it works once in a lifetime, that's enough.

That's how I found out that 35 percent of their business came from one customer. Something I'd always suspected – but not to the tune of 35 percent – something it would have taken a year for me, their most hated competitor, to pry out of them if I'd started to deal directly with them at the outset.

LESSON 22

There is no such thing as a sold-out house

Did you ever have to negotiate a hotel room?

I'm never able to plan a vacation very far in advance, but I've never been shut out, even in Acapulco a week before Christmas. Here's how you do it. You call. Mexico. Wherever. Not a travel agent or a secretary. You. The reservations clerk tells you no. Get his name. Then you say, 'Look, you have five-hundred rooms and five-hundred reservations. I know, and you know, somebody out of those five-hundred people isn't going to show up. Somebody will get sick. Somebody won't be able to interrupt a big business deal. Whatever. With five-hundred people it has to happen. We just don't know *who* it's going to happen to be. So all I'm asking is not that you give me a reservation but that you put my name on the top of the waiting list, and because I'm so sure that there's going to be an opening, I'm sending the money, in advance, and you can be sure that when you call me collect and tell me there's an opening, and I come down there, I'll remember you exactly one hundred ways.' Then give your name and number, hang up the phone, and wire the reservation money. They always call back.

LESSON 23

Understanding your banker

Visiting the banker always makes the list of life's sweaty-palmed experiences. Stripping down to have your financials examined is submitting to an emotional proctoscopy that no amount of 'friendly banker' advertising is ever going to change. There's a reason these meetings take place on the banker's turf, in buildings designed as Temples of Commerce. Lest we forget, money is a subject to be taken very seriously.

But bankers are people with a product to sell. Money. It is a wasting asset. When it sits in T-bills, which is where it is when it isn't being lent out, it earns 5 percent. When it's invested in your mortgage or your car, it's earning at least twice that much. Even with a default rate of 2½ percent – what the very worst banks experience – they still earn a hell of a lot more when it's loaned out than when it isn't. Here's how a wealthy German industrialist negotiated with his banker.

Herr Schwan, we will call him, was well into his seventies but still active in business. He learned that his son, who fancied himself a real-estate developer, had gotten in well over his head on an apartment project. The senior Schwan had no desire to put in his own money. He decided to borrow it. So he had his bookkeeper, the formidable Frau Hoffman, make an appointment for them with a banker, Herr Wittman. Schwan and Hoffman arrived at the banker's desk at

the hour Herr Schwan selected: four-thirty on Friday afternoon. Schwan had done his homework here, too. He selected the right bank, the right time, and the right banker. He
knew Wittman had two passions: tennis and opera.

As the meeting started with the customary small talk,
Schwan, who had never been particularly talkative before,
began to hold forth. First: tennis – he competed at Wimble-
don once, 1931, first round. The long-forgotten match was
reprised. Next, opera. Highlights of four decades of Wagner
festivals at Bayreuth were recalled. The clock struck the
hour. Time for good bank employees to clear their desks
and go home. Herr Wittman, a compulsive clean-desk type,
nervously fingered the 'Schwan' file on his desk. He had
expected to reach an agreement with Schwan that afternoon – and be able to report it to his superiors at their
regular weekly meeting on Monday morning. Herr Schwan
droned on.

At five-ten, Herr Schwan rose from his chair, looked at
his watch, and said how much he enjoyed his chat, but he
was expected elsewhere. Wittman helped him struggle into
his coat, but it was not until Schwan and Hoffman turned
their backs and headed for the elevator that the first word
of the purpose of the meeting was mentioned – by the
banker.

'You did want to discuss something about a mortgage,
Herr Schwan?' says Wittman.

'Mortgage? You wanted me to see him about a mortgage,
Frau Hoffman?' said Schwan. This whole business was, of
course, Frau Hoffman's idea.

Schwan never requested a loan. Wittman brought up the
subject; it was left to Wittman to make the offer. He did,
while they were still on their feet, standing by the elevator
doors.

The interest rate charged was 6.18 percent. The bank
should have gotten at least 7. And the terms were fantastic!

'I remember the deal perfectly,' said his other son, who
did not get himself involved in shaky real-estate deals.

'Because, of course, my father, despite giving a bravura performance as an absentminded old man, faultlessly reiterated every detail.'

Absentminded, indeed!

Don't forget, despite all the psychological barriers they throw at you, that the banker is the seller; you are the buyer. They don't make house calls, but that doesn't mean your job is to persuade them to do business with you. Their job is to persuade *you*. Make them do it. You'll get a better deal.

The single most powerful tool for winning a negotiation is the ability to walk away from the table without a deal

Herr Schwan demonstrated that walking away from the table is not just for when you *don't* want to deal. Sometimes it's the only way you can make the deal you want.

If you *have* to have a deal, then all the other side needs to do to win the negotiation is to outwait you.

Take international relations. It used to be assumed that being bamboozled in treaty negotiations was part of the price of a free society. The reason the democracies have been such failures in international negotiations with tyrannies is that the attitudes of the general public are part of the baggage our representatives bring to the bargaining table – and the general public has an expectation that 'success' in bargaining is measured by the act of reaching an agreement, never mind what the agreement is.

As a result, once our foreign-policymakers are maneuvered into going into negotiations, it's almost inevitable that we lose, because the other side knows that they have only to refuse to make a deal – unless it's one they regard as favorable to them – and the public perception will be that our negotiators will have lost a key opportunity.

Vyacheslav Molotov, the longtime foreign minister of the

Soviet Union, was so adept at this outwaiting technique that his nickname was 'Ironpants'.

Well, things have changed. For one thing, strikes are no longer automatically settled on the unions' terms. Though the air-traffic controllers' strike proved that in 1981, it took the Hormel meatpackers' strike in 1986 to convince some of the slow learners.

And in foreign policy, we no longer make concessions on demand. In fact, we've been known to get up and walk away when the deal isn't to our liking.

Don't let the message be lost on you: Whether it's a labor negotiation, an acquisition, or a real-estate deal, don't deceive yourself into believing that just because it's negotiable it has to be negotiated.

I had occasion to take my own advice recently. Five partners had formed a real-estate deal to develop a major hotel property in Chicago. Two days before all the financial commitments were to be signed and the bank was to issue their letter of credit, one of the partners, an architect, dropped out in a dispute over the dollar value they'd be credited with for their professional work. That's when they contacted me. I was offered very attractive terms and given twenty-four hours to make up my mind. When the time was up, I said, 'Thank you very much. It's a very attractive deal. But I still haven't decided that I want to take it.' And I left the table. The next day – after the ironclad twenty-four-hour deadline had expired – the phone rang and the terms got even more attractive, including a guarantee by a financial angel with *Forbes* 400 net worth that eliminated any downside risk.

Deals seldom get worse when you walk away from the table.

Be prepared to walk away from the table . . . and mean it. You'll be able to go back to the table and get even better terms.

LESSON 25

'Calling Mr. Otis'

You say you'll not likely be called on to negotiate Salt II, or handle the company's real-estate or labor contracts? No matter. You're still going to find yourself in the midst of a negotiation where your ability to get up and walk away is the key to winning.

There's an ancient scam in the car business known as 'Calling Mr. Otis'. The prospect comes in and to his great surprise is given a fabulous offer for his old beater trade-in and an even better deal on his new car purchase. He shops around, finds the deal is unbeatable, and comes back to the dealer with the terrific proposition.

The salesperson writes up the deal. He has the prospect initial it. Then he asks the prospect casually what the other dealers offered him. At this point, the prospect, flushed with victory, tosses away the most valuable asset he has in the negotiation: information – to wit, the other dealers' prices.

'Just one last step,' says the salesperson. 'The sales manager has to okay the deal. I'll call him right now.' The salesperson punches the intercom device on his phone and says, "Calling Mr. Otis . . . calling Mr. Otis." Of course, there is no Mr. Otis. There's a sales manager, all right, but his name is really Smith or Jones or whatever.

Otis is the name of the company that makes elevators – and this elevator is going up. The sales manager shows up.

He pulls the salesman out of the room to let the prospect stew for a while, the salesman comes back, says Otis won't go for the deal, and then proceeds to retrade it up to exactly the same level as the other dealers had offered the prospect. Why, you might ask, doesn't the prospect simply walk at this point?

Because he has too much invested emotionally in cutting the deal right there; he's already picked out his new car. It's blue with red upholstery and it's sitting right there on the showroom floor, waiting for him to drive it off. While he's in the closing room with the salesman, his wife is sitting behind the wheel and his kids are jumping up and down on the seats. He's told everybody at work what a shrewd negotiator he is.

If he *doesn't* sign his name, he has to pick up and start all over again . . . the kids will start crying . . . again; and they'll snicker at him down at work . . . again.

So what's $870.50 more on a $15,000 purchase? Just a few more monthly payments. This is America, pal, thanks a lot, have a nice day, and here's your payment book. He signs because he can't walk away from the table without a deal. But you can. And when you do, you'll end up buying your cars for less money than you would if you fell for this classic scam.

LESSON 26

The most important term in any contract isn't in the contract

It's dealing with people who are honest.

The second most important term is including the right to inspect all their books and records, including tax records, correspondence, etc., pertaining to the agreement. Once *that* clause is in there, people with a tendency to get cute usually don't.

LESSON 27

Agreements prevent disagreements

Every now and then you'll find yourself dealing with one of those country cousin types who says he doesn't want a contract and 'your word is good enough.' Maybe yours is, but his usually isn't.

One of those arrangements taught me a lesson I'll never forget. I had a handshake deal with a man I hired. He agreed that he would not seek other employment for two years. After a year, a better offer came along, and he was gone. He said that he remembered that we had agreed on only one year. How could I prove he was wrong? I couldn't. Now what I do when I make a deal with one of these country cousins is send a letter *that same day* in which I

1. thank him profusely for his courtesy and

2. set out the terms of the deal: 'As I understand our agreement, I have agreed to. . . .'

I don't usually ask for any acknowledgment (though you could just to be on the safe side – to make sure the letter arrived). It's just a nice, friendly little letter – and a useful record if there should be any misunderstandings later.

LESSON 28

The longer they keep you waiting, the more they want to deal

This isn't mine: I read it in an article in *The New York Times*. The fellow who said this knows what he's talking about. He's Leslie H. Wexner, chairman of The Limited, one of the most successful new retail chains. He illustrates the point with a story about Meshulam Riklis, who made it big putting together Rapid American Corporation. They had scheduled a major negotiating session in Wexner's office. Wexner is the buyer; Riklis is the seller. Riklis shows up two hours late with his wife, Pia Zadora, in tow and explains that he was delayed because she wanted to go antique shopping. Anyone who goes to that much trouble to try to show you how much he *doesn't* care if he sells something cares a hell of a lot more than he's willing to admit. The harder he tries to conceal his eagerness to unload, the bigger the rug he has to put it under. Wexner got a better deal than he had hoped for.

I had a similar experience. As head of a trade delegation to China, I was responsible for seeing to it that some very elaborate formal brochures we'd prepared were distributed to our Chinese counterparts. The brochures were beautifully bound in blue vellum and contained detailed descriptions of the members of our delegation, our backgrounds, and our capabilities. I was proud of them, knew they contained information that would be useful to the Chinese, and wanted to pass them out, but our hosts said, 'Don't worry. We'll pass them out at the right time.' The right time never came as the Chinese made a great show of not being terribly interested. I just couldn't understand why they didn't even care to glance at our knockout brochures. So I 'accidentally' left them behind after our discussions one day. When I came back five minutes later to retrieve them, they were poring through them – with much clucking and gesturing and with great smiles on their faces when I caught them at it.

The Soviets are masters of using timing to wear down and throw off an adversary across the negotiation table. In a study for the Rand Corporation, Thane Gustafson wrote about East-West bargaining that ultimately set the stage for the gas pipeline deal:

'A West European gas executive recalls that in 1974, "on the last night of a fruitless and frustrating trip to Moscow, we were dining glumly at the Arbat Restaurant. Suddenly, at eleven o'clock, Osipov [the Soviet negotiator] swept in, commandeered a private dining room, and right there, through the small hours of the morning, we hammered out the contract."'

Beware the late dealer. Unless you are on your guard, you may read his intentions totally wrong and end up giving up a bargaining advantage. Feigning indifference or casually desregarding timetables is often just a shrewd negotiator's way to make *you* believe he doesn't care.

LESSON 29

He who burns his bridges better be a damn good swimmer

Real-estate operators are legendary for slow-pay practices, but I know one who hangs them all out to dry. This gentleman – we'll call him 'Bob' – was the son of a milkman. He made a fortune in the trucking business and wound up owning major league sports franchises on both coasts. To give you an idea of how nimble he was, after he bought his first sports franchise in the Midwest, he also bought – quietly and cheaply – an obscure FM radio station on the West Coast. In a big surprise move, he then shifted the franchise to the Coast and scheduled the game broadcasts exclusively on his new station. Moving not only revived the failing franchise, it also multiplied the value of the station. One move. Two profits.

Bob also owned a chain of hotels. A large, sophisticated New York insurance company held the mortgage on his flagship hotel. One Friday, the insurance company in question, exasperated over years of delayed payments or no payments, sent their man to see Bob. The intrepid rep marched into Bob's office, threw down a sheaf of legal papers, and announced that as of Monday, the insurance company would take over and operate the hotel.

'That's fine,' said Bob, 'but where will you park the guests' cars?'

'Why, in the parking lot behind the hotel,' said the insurance company's man.

87

'No,' said he, 'you won't be parking them there. I *own* that parking lot. The minute you take over the hotel, an eight-foot chain link fence goes around that lot, and in case you haven't noticed, there isn't another adequate parking facility you can use within a three-block radius.'

The New York insurance company decided it could live with Bob's payment practices.

LESSON 30

Make your decisions with your heart, and what you'll end up with is heart disease

I have always been passionate about sports, as you may have gathered by now. I also love to manage. So when the opportunity came along a few years back to own a professional sports team in a brand-new sports league, they nearly had to put me in restraints to keep me from signing up.

This was the deal: In 1971, a group of prominent businessmen got together to launch a new sports concept, the International Basketball League – the IBL.

International communications were in their infancy. The age of Marshall McLuhan's 'Global Village' was dawning. Sports were a vivid, enduring symbol of international brotherhood. And here was I – destined to become a Founding Father of global sports for Planet Earth!

The plan was to take the sport of basketball and transplant an NBA-style league first to Europe and the Middle East . . . and then doubtless to all four corners of the world. Imagine it: From Samoa to Smolensk, the world would be ringed with one huge basketball hoop.

Phase I was to create franchises in eight cities: Rome, Amsterdam, Madrid, Munich, Tel Aviv, Geneva, Brussels, and Düsseldorf, and I was fantasizing journeying off to

Germany — munching a wurst and sipping Alt Bier as I strolled down Düsseldorf's posh Königsallee, fantasizing myself as Europe's Baron von Basketball.

When the time had come, the organizers gathered the propects together in a huge hall in Houston. We were wined and dined like international dignitaries. The room was charged, there were spotlights and microphones everywhere. It was like a marriage of the UN Security Council and the college football draft.

There were speeches, there was hoopla. There were promises of glory and riches. Then there was the setting of the hook — a hook I had seen set countless times at fundraising dinners before. The price for involvement, for being part of the dream, was a no-recourse down payment of $250,000. Around the room the spotlight went: 'Madrid pledges $250,000,' 'Munich pledges $250,000.' Finally they came to Düsseldorf, and my heart was in my mouth. The mandarins of the mighty IBL had set a table from which it was all but impossible to walk away. There was emotional and physical exhaustion after weeks of head-splitting negotiations. There was the disorientation of living in strange hotel rooms in exotic settings followed by exotic hotel rooms in strange settings. There was peer pressure. There was guilt. There was pride. It was like a fund-raiser where everyone else in the room has announced their pledge — except you — and now every eyeball in the place is boring into your skull.

The emcee at the microphone repeated the question softly but with intensity: 'Düsseldorf. May we have Düsseldorf's pledge.'

It's your turn, pal.

I want to say yes. I have to say yes.

But I say, 'Düsseldorf passes.'

And do you know what happened?

Nothing happened.

The world did not stop spinning on its axis. There was the predictable flurry of whispering and head-shaking across the room. I had flinched at the firing line.

Why had I passed? Passed. When everything seemed so right. When it was something I so dearly wanted. The truth is, I distrusted the *mechanism* for getting commitments. It made me suspicious of the entire plan.

As it turned out, my gut was right. The IBL folded after one season of play. Each franchisee lost as much as $1 million in the process.

Now, sometimes worthy causes, fully deserving of support, raise money in this way. The cause may be worthy, but in my opinion, the method never is. You have not only the right, but also the personal responsibility to think in a cool and calm way about any major investment you are asked to make. Never make a significant deal that is proposed to you, a deal that is going to involve your commitment to spend your own money, on the spur of the moment. There is no more certain recipe for disaster than a decision based on emotion.

You may never get trapped in a lavish hotel suite with seven other sports-mad businessmen hungry for status on the international scene, but somewhere along the line something similar is going to happen to you. Someone is going to say this is absolutely your last chance to accept their generous offer. Someone is going to make you an offer you can't refuse. Where every step has been choreographed, every note orchestrated to lead up to that one moment, the moment when it's your cue, your duty, your responsibility, to say yes.

Say no.

LESSON 31

Never buy anything in a room with a chandelier

In case my IBL experience doesn't persuade you, here's a story by an old politician that will illustrate my point.

The time is the winter of 1967-68. The scene is the O'Hare Inn near Chicago. Fifty or sixty GOP operatives are meeting. They are Nixon supporters, many of them nationally known, including Senators Everett Dirksen and Hiram Fong, Governor John Lodge, former Congressman Bo Callaway, and the presider-over, a future attorney general, Richard Kleindienst. They are gathered to plot strategy and count delegates . . . and simply, by showing up together in the same room, hype each other with the strength of Nixon's developing effort to capture the nomination in Miami, six months away.

It's an impressive showing. There's a mock roll call of the states, where, unsurprisingly, Nixon wins on the first ballot (which, surprisingly, he later actually did). Kleindienst plugs into Nixon in New York, and via speakerphone, Nixon gives a little pep talk, which reaches its crescendo in a promise that, when he's elected, everyone in the audience would have 'jobs'. It's the biggest applause line of the day, though the appeal of jobs to United States senators, who already had pretty good ones, seems hard to fathom.

The meeting adjourns.

Most people leave. My friend, who was a small-time operative running a small-time portion of the campaign that focused on volunteer groups, trailed after Bud Wilkinson, a former head football coach at Oklahoma and an unsuccessful GOP candidate for senator from that state, to a remote suite at the inn for further instructions.

There were all the biggies from the meeting, including Kleindienst. Taking further refreshment and holding forth in one corner was a congressman who later became a cabinet member in the Nixon administration.

The congressman speaks:

'In every national campaign, there is a special office, usually right in the center of the country, here in Chicago.

'The office has to have a chandelier. That's critical. This has to be one very impressive office.

'There's a big desk and seated behind the desk is someone who appears to be the candidate's innermost, closest, most trusted adviser.

'And every day during the campaign, people come to that office and bring money.

'Not really big money.

'Not Dallas money.

'Medium money.

'And they tell the trusted adviser what it is they want, because nobody gives anybody money in America without wanting something in return. Usually it's to be an ambassador or an under secretary.

'Now, medium money wouldn't get you into the ambassador's pantry in Sri Lanka, but you can't dump on people who give you money just because they don't know how the world works.

'So the man behind the desk . . . nods gravely and takes notes on a beautiful Mark Cross pad.

'The donor goes away. He's happy. He can tell his wife and his friends he talked to the next president's brother. He'll even get a beautiful copy of a letter on fancy stationery that the brother sends to the candidate, talking about

Joe Suitcase's 'deep commitment' or 'very deep commitment' to our tiger's candidacy. And best of all, we can forget about him, because anyone dumb enough to let himself get steered to that office in Chicago with the chandelier isn't worth worrying about later on, just in case we do win the presidency.'

We've all heard it said that if any proposition looks too good to be true, it probably is. But before you decide to invest, look beyond the proposition itself, and

- If the surroundings are too grand
- If there are too many unfamiliar faces
- If it is too far away from home
- If the people are too nice
- If the business is too glamorous
- If the title that comes with your participation is too elegant – in other words, even if the proposition seems right, but if considered in the context of all these other factors, it all seems a little too much, my friend, just remember these two magic words: DÜSSELDORF PASSES.

Then grab your checkbook and get the hell out of there.

LESSON 32

Everything's negotiable

Within the past few years, some of the best-known names in American industry, like Gulf Oil, American Broadcasting, and Montgomery Ward, have disappeared down the gaping maws of other companies. Other seemingly unassailable fortresses, like AT&T, have been disassembled and the parts sold off separately. Nothing unusual about that. Capitalism, by definition, is a system in which everything is for sale.

If huge enterprises, some so valuable their assets exceed those of most of the nations in the world, can be bought and sold, cut up into little pieces, or put together into bigger pieces, like a heap of scrap iron, then there's no deal that you and I could contemplate that can't be put together. A deal can *always* be made when the parties see it to their own benefit.

Nine out of ten lawsuits are settled before judgment is rendered in the courtroom because even the bitterest of adversaries will sit down at the same table when they can be shown there is a greater advantage to themselves in negotiating than in fighting.

Whatever it is you are trying to buy or sell can be bought or sold if you can get the other side of the table to see how the deal works to their advantage.

It's said that when Moses came down from the mountain

after getting the Ten Commandments, he said, 'Well, we reasoned together. I got Him down to ten, but adultery's still in.'

LESSON 33

The buyer/seller battle

In the war between big-hat sellers and buyers, the seller uses the weapons of the offense:

- reconnaissance, through devices like the 'Mackay 66'
- infiltration, concocting personality and even ethnic matchups between seller and buyer
- propaganda, through advertising and PR
- shifting tactics, probing for the weaknesses in the buyers' defenses, that one yes, that one telltale clue that will open up the lines
- persistence, pressure, and ultimatum

The buyer uses the weapons of the defense:

- reconnaissance, through buffers like clones (see page 73)
- time, a tactic which also includes the use of distance, evasion, confusion, humor – anything that will increase the buyer's pool of information and exhaust the seller into conceding more favorable terms
- minor skirmishes, testing the waters to win concessions . . . and again, wearing out the seller
- ambushes, last-minute ultimatums to wring major concessions after the seller thinks he has a deal and is already mentally counting out and counting on the profit

About an equal matchup, isn't it? Who wins? Same as always: the player with the better information, the better plan, and greater skill.

Chapter IV

HARVEY MACKAY'S SHORT COURSE IN MANAGEMENT

◆

LESSON 34

The single greatest mistake a manager can make

You don't have to be a tyrant to get Americans to work together. Hitler's notion of what the American character is all about was gleaned from his reading of Western novels by Karl May, books that every German boy was brought up on, by a man who'd never set foot in the United States. But that didn't stop Hitler from holding an unshakable opinion about the United States and how it worked. Looking at the barrage of competing ideas that spring from our tolerance of free expression, Hitler saw what he assumed must be total chaos. He envisioned a disorganized society and, as a result, one that was weak, vulnerable, and uncommitted to any sustained effort.

I remember that one of my most exciting experiences as a boy came during World War II when my dad arranged to take me along on an airplane filled with reporters to watch a big contest between Minneapolis and St. Paul. It was to see which could black out its city faster in an air raid alert practice. The plane flew along the border between the two cities, and I pressed my face as hard as I could against the window so I wouldn't miss anything. When the air raid signal sounded, the lights went out as if an unseen hand had flicked off a single switch.

Hitler found out that Americans of every variety of opinion and background can pull together. You just have to give us a reason.

That's what managers are supposed to be able to provide.

Motivation. Goals. Resources. Leadership. But *not* restrictions. *Not* being told what to do. *Not* rules. Oh, God, how Americans hate rules. One of the sharpest entrepreneurs ever was Gardner Symonds, a former chairman of Tenneco. Tenneco people describe Symonds as the person who had the vision to make Tenneco what it is today – a $14 billion company. I had dinner with him once when he spoke at a seminar at Stanford.

He said there are four things you need to do to build a successful business. One: Find the capital. Two: Find a favorable environment to employ it. Three: Hire the key people. And here's where he took a long pause and said, 'So far, I'm not telling you anything you didn't already know, because number four is the important one. Then you've got to know *when* to get the hell out of the way. That's the hardest part, but that's the one that will make you rich.'

I have a friend, Pat Fallon, who runs an advertising agency. Within three years of the time he opened his shop, *Advertising Age* named Fallon McElligott Rice as Agency of the Year, the equivalent of sweeping the Academy Awards. It was an unheard-of honor for an agency that new, and one located neither in New York or L.A. but in the 'fly-over land' of the Midwest.

Fallon's management style is ideal for the fragile creative egos he handles. They're not exactly dress-code types. If he tried to enforce a white-shirt rule, the place would empty out in fifteen minutes. But he has the same problem everyone in the business has: getting out a superior product. He does it by maximizing personal freedom and thus personal responsibility to an almost unheard-of extent.

A PR fellow I know who worked for him at another agency said, 'I was there two years before I even knew Fallon was my boss, and that was only because he left, and the guy who replaced him told me I'd be reporting to him instead of Fallon from then on.'

Fallon understands that in *his* business – and in yours, more than you realize – what people are looking for isn't only money, it's recognition, appreciation, and creative freedom. He gives them what they need. They give him what he needs: the best product in the industry.

Fallon doesn't give orders; he facilitates the creative process by hard work and accessibility. In the ad game, your inventory is ideas, and they can come from anyone, anywhere. Art directors are as capable of great copy as copy-writers are of graphic concepts. The key to keeping the ideas flowing is an atmosphere where everyone can feel free to contribute. That atmosphere requires a barrier-free environment. That's why if you pick up the phone and call Fallon, you get Fallon . . . without anyone asking who you are or what you want. There aren't many $100 million-a-year businesses where you can get the boss on the phone without passing through a receptionist and three secretaries. Though Fallon probably talks to more insurance agents and stockbrokers than he wants to, it's a small price to pay for creating the best advertising agency in the country.

No matter what business you're in, to be successful, managers must create the kind of environment that makes their people the most productive. It isn't enough to make them conscious of details if you destroy their sense of freedom and spontaneity in the process. You must understand them well enough to give them not what *you* want, but also what *they* need to make a maximum contribution.

Look at the people who walk out *your* door and leave you

101

to become successful at their own businesses. Chances are they're not doing it just for the money. They need the room to express their own styles. Give them that room . . . and the recognition and appreciation . . . and nine out of ten times they won't leave. We've been hearing a lot about 'intrapreneurship' lately. But it isn't some new form of capitalism. It's the old idea of taking talented men or women one step short of a full partnership, a means for making the employee president of his own company rather than losing him.

We have a sharp young person in our firm who could easily have been a great success on his own, and he had reached the point where he realized it. Just in time, we furnished him the capital and the infrastructure to manufacture his own speciality line as president of Minnesota Colour Envelope Company, a Mackay Envelope subsidiary. Sure, it's not as profitable for us as it would have been if he'd been content to stay on as an ordinary employee. But that wasn't the alternative. The alternative was losing him and winding up having him as a competitor.

Lyndon Johnson provided the ultimate justification for that kind of 'intrapreneurship', albeit a negative one, in describing his relationship with J. Edgar Hoover: 'I'd rather have him inside the tent pissing out than outside the tent pissing in.'

So remember, you can get your employees to pay attention to detail, and run your ship like an America's Cup yacht, if you develop a leadership style that delivers your message in a positive way, and if you demonstrate your confidence in your people by giving them freedom to do the job you hired them to do.

Be like jockey Willie Shoemaker. He's the best in the business because he has the lightest touch on the reins. They say the horse never knows he's there – unless he's needed.

LESSON 35

When a person with money meets a person with experience, the person with the experience winds up with the money and the person with the money winds up with the experience

When I bought – or rather, when I was dumb enough to get stuck with – an envelope company, it had twelve employees, sales of $200,000 annually, and a sackful of nuts and bolts that passed for envelope-making equipment. I thought I was being very businesslike when I asked to see the books. 'Forget the books, sonny,' my charming predecessor said. 'Take it or leave it.'

When I said I'd take it, the lawyer I had hired to advise me in this transaction quit. For the first five years I teetered between bankruptcy and insanity.

Nothing I learned during those years about the envelope business was as valuable as what I learned about lawyers and accountants. Lawyers and accountants make excellent lawyers and accountants. They're great specialists in what they do, but you might as well rely on a paediatrician for specific business advice.

I also learned something about dealing with that great American institution, the labor movement.

At the end of year one, my employees, sensing that

perhaps I was not going into the tank after all, began to answer the siren song of the labor movement. Before they could take a vote, I called my new lawyer and asked him what I could do.

'Harvey,' he said, 'you can't fire them for considering a union, and you can't threaten them. That would be an unfair labor practice. But you can call them into the office, one at a time, and tell them of the great progress that they'll make if only we can all strive for a common goal, without outside interference telling us how to run our business, and so on.'

And so that's what I did.

One at a time, I called them into the office. One at a time, I took them to the top of the mountain and described the glorious landscape that lay at our feet if only we could continue to work together in the future as we had in the past. And one at a time, my twenty employees told me that as a result of my stirring speech, he or she would cast their vote against the union.

That is, all except one employee. He said, 'Mr. Mackay, my grandfather was a union man, my dad was a union man, and I'm a union man, and I'm voting union.'

There it was. I was going to win, nineteen to one. With surprising ease, in my very first attempt, at the still-wet-behind-the-ears age of twenty-six, I had proved myself a born master of labor relations.

This was too easy. I was an entrepreneur! I couldn't wait to call my lawyer. He seemed somewhat restrained in his praise, but I took that to be the result of a touch of jealousy at my having shown such natural aptitude for a skill it had taken him years to perfect. 'Call me *after* the vote,' he said.

The next day they held the election. Sure enough, the vote was nineteen to one – in *favor* of the union! I'd lost, nineteen to one; they'd handed me my head. This was not the way I'd learned it in Labor Relations 101.

What I did learn was that I had to be ready to make very rapid midcourse corrections in small things to keep my major business objectives intact. Or, as my father taught me, 'It doesn't matter how many pails of milk you spill, just so you don't lose the cow.' The end of the story is that I raised my prices so I could afford union wages.

In the years since I learned those lessons and took my first bumbling steps in business, Mackay Envelope has grown to over 350 employees, sales of approximately $35 million, and modern plants in both Minnesota and Iowa.

It's a nice little 'only in America' story and I'm going to tell you how I did it – and how you can do exactly the same thing. Note, first of all, that we're not talking about an idiotproof business. Mackay Envelope did not prosper because there was a shift in the economy in favor of the envelope industry, nor did I uncover the perfect product at the perfect time or carve out a new market niche. Envelopes fall under the classic definition of a mature industry, à la steel and cement. Our products are constantly being assaulted by sexier, more convenient means of communication, like telephones and computers. To increase revenues, the successful envelope entrepreneur has but one logical strategy: take the market share from someone else. That means salesmanship and the ability to manage a business where margins can be wafer-thin and you can barely tell your own products from your competitor's. Unlike farming, you can't even get the politicians sufficiently interested to make speeches saying you're the backbone of the American way of life. The envelope game seems to lack the glamor and visibility of higher callings like these, so what I've learned, I've learned by getting slam-dunked often enough until the message sunk in.

LESSON 36

You'll always get the good news; it's how quickly you get the bad news that counts

I have one ironclad rule for myself. I walk my plant every day just like it says in *In Search of Excellence*. I can learn something new and get the feel, touch, and pulse of the place without anyone having to say a single word to me. Without a single word? Absolutely. Do wives and husbands have to announce each other's moods with a drum roll and trumpet fanfare?

A capable manager walks his plant and gets the good news before anyone else.

An outstanding manager gets the bad news first. Nobody wants to be the bearer of bad tidings, because that triggers the kill-the-messenger syndrome. If you're in charge, you have to *encourage* the flow of bad news, because if you don't bad situations get worse – before you can stop the hemorrhaging.

If your only means of communicating upward is a formal, operations-manual kind of system, you're making a mistake. Don't rely on the formal chain of command to provide you with the bad news. If there's a problem, the manager in that area will always try to solve it before you hear about it. He'll justify his action as being within his scope of responsibility, but he'll be motivated as much by a sense of wanting to cover it up before you hear about it.

You need a second line of communications. You have to encourage not only your own people, but your customers, too, to talk to you informally, to feel comfortable approaching you in the halls and getting concerns off their chests.

One of the largest and most successful retailers in the world is the Dayton Hudson Corporation. There is no tougher business. Look at some of the retail giants that have gone under, American institutions like W. T. Grant and Gimbles Stores, or that have gotten into trouble, like Abercrombie & Fitch, Wickes, Montgomery Ward, Daylin, and Kennedy and Cohen.

How have the Dayton brothers managed to survive and succeed where so many others have failed? For many years, you could ask Don Dayton, but the place to find him was not in his office. It was out on the floor of his store. When he did go to his eleventh-floor office, it was never by elevator. Don took the escalator. He could see more of what was going on that way. According to Ken Macke, Dayton Hudson CEO, every major executive at Dayton's still goes up and down those eleven floors the same way every day — by escalator. That isn't just walking the store. That's minding the store. The mark of a real pro, no matter what the business, is recognizing that the absolutely best business information you can get is never found in a report or other secondhand information. It's a steady diet of nose-to-nose, constant, immediate, unfiltered feedback from your customers and employees.

LESSON 37

Throw it on the floor

I have a very simple way of making sure that a job I really don't want to do gets done. I write out a brief description on a sheet of yellow legal paper and throw the paper on the floor next to my desk. To get to my desk, I have to go through the nuisance of stepping around, over, or on it. Whatever it is, it gets done in a hurry. Genius may not always be equated with messiness, but the following words are very much to the point:

Picture yourself the darkest, most disorderly place imaginable . . . blotches of moisture covered the ceiling; an oldish grand piano, on which the dust disputed the place with various pieces of engraved and manuscript music; under the piano (I do not exaggerate) an unemptied chamber pot; beside it a small walnut table accustomed to the frequent overturning of the secretary placed on it; a quantity of pens encrusted with ink, compared with which the proverbial tavern pens would shine; then more music. The chairs, mostly cane-seated, were covered with plates bearing the remains of last night's supper, and with wearing apparel, etc.

That passage is found in *The Lives of the Great Composers*, by Harold C. Schonberg. It is Baron de Tremont's description of Beethoven's 'office'.

LESSON 38

Treat your suppliers the way you treat your customers

Despite the fancy fruit baskets at Christmastime and the expense account lunches, most of us think of suppliers like the old *U.S. Navy Officers' Manual* description of enlisted men: 'They are ignorant, but they are shrewd. They bear watching at all times.'

The Billy Graham organization takes a different approach, one that's a lot closer to the Golden Rule than it is to the *Navy Manual*. For one thing, suppliers don't always have to bid for their business; BG doesn't necessarily base supply decisions on meeting specs. Here's an example of how they do it.

A friend of mine, let's call him Al, is in the public-relations business. He serves as an outside adviser on a church board public-relations committee. He's a friend of the pastor and such an indefatigable PR type that he does it for the fun of it even though he doesn't belong to the church and is hardly what I would call religious. Another member of the same advisory board is an officer of the Graham organization. Let's call him Arthur.

It so happened that Al was loudly and publicly fired from his job. There was no way any other firm in town would hire him, so he opened up an office on his own. About three weeks after opening his doors, and mostly twiddling his thumbs, he received a call from Arthur at BG. Until then, Al had never seen Arthur outside the board meetings. Arthur asked whether he would have time to help develop a marketing plan and some PR materials for one of their campaigns. Al managed to find the time. When he had completed the project, Arthur asked Al to bring over his bill. Al thought that was kind of curious – most people expect you to mail it in – but he figured, well, they want to go over it with me. So Al nervously put together his statement very carefully, itemized everything, and went over.

Arthur barely glanced at it. He called his secretary in and said, 'Will you see if we can cut Al's check right now.' And, of course, they did. He was paid before he left the building.

Where do they tell you in business school to pay your suppliers when they hand you the bill? Aren't we supposed to hang on to our cash as long as possible and work the interest for the maximum return? Did anyone you know ever chew out his controller because he paid a supplier too late?

There's a little more to the story. It's Christmastime three years later. Al's business has taken off; he's thriving. He did several more major jobs for BG, but as he got busier, he didn't hear much from them anymore. The phone rings. It's Arthur. Would Al like 'a little extra holiday money'? They have a job that needs his immediate personal attention. By this time Al has ten employees. He's trying to hire two more that week and they're up to their ears in work. 'I told him I was really as busy as I had ever been,' said Al, 'but if they really wanted my help, of course, I'd be happy to do it. Or even give them the name of someone else who could help.' 'No,' Arthur says, 'I'll take care of it. Thanks anyway. Glad you're doing so well.'

'We talked for a little while more, just chit chat stuff, but when I hung up the phone, I started to shake, and then I started to cry. All those jobs I'd done before, all the business he had given me when I was sitting there by myself. The nagging suspicion I'd had from the beginning was confirmed. It wasn't because I was such a great PR guy. There are many in town who could have done it better. They knew the territory a lot better than I did. But Arthur asked me because they knew I was hurting, and I needed the business. And then they called me again, just checking in, kind of, to see if I still needed help. Nobody I've ever done business with before has ever cared about me the way the Billy Graham organization did. And I'm Jewish.'

That afternoon, Al sent them a nice big contribution. He still sends them checks every year, and he hasn't done business with them in years. BG had cared about him when it counted; he has never forgotten it. And he never will. How many companies can say they have made *permanent* customers out of their suppliers long after they ceased to furnish supplies? By helping him when he needed it, BG earned loyalty that no amount of money could buy. BG has recognized a business principle that is so elementary, so corny, that we seldom ever use it: If you expect the other guy to care about you, show that you care about him. Sounds pretty close to that Golden Rule business again, but does it ever work for BG. What kind of service do you think BG gets? What kind of reputation do they have in the community? What kind of prices and delivery do they get from their suppliers?

I can answer all of the above because I'm another supplier, and a Jewish one, too, that the Billy Graham organization helped get started in business. They get the best quality. They get the best delivery. They get the best prices . . . you can be certain that they *know* what they should be paying even though they don't get bids for their outside needs. If you overcharge, you still get paid, *once*, and then you never hear from them again. And, of course, because they pay so promptly, you don't have to build an annoyance or cost-of-money factor into your billing. Simply stated, they are regarded as the finest account in town, not just because of the way they pay – I've gotten paid many times before I shipped, absolutely unheard-of in the envelope business – but also because of the quality of the people at BG. In fact, we're willing to take less just for the privilege of doing business with them.

The way you pay your bills says something about the kind of person you are to deal with. Whether it's the man who painted your house or the firm that delivers your raw stock, you'll always get a better shake if you pay the same day you get the bill.

LESSON 39

The time for the Renaissance man was the Renaissance

The success of the Graham organization is a reflection of two very different talents: Billy Graham himself and George Wilson. Billy is the quintessential Mr. Outside. He embodies the image of the organization both to the outside world and to the people who work at BG. His character, his leadership, his enormous public presence, and his following are at the heart of the tremendous morale that surrounds the place, even though it is so inconspicuous you can barely find the sign on the door. While Billy provides the inspiration, George keeps the place humming. He's Mr. Inside: low-profile, low-key, tireless, with an eye for talent and detail, with an easygoing, warm, one-on-one style and absolutely committed to Billy and running an efficient, modern operation.

Most organizations and especially manufacturing companies need both these talents: the salesman who brings in the business and the manager who knows what to do with it. But you'd be surprised how many businesses there are where they either don't understand that those two talents seldom run together in the same person or where destructive conflicts between the inside types and outside types end up tearing the place apart.

The New York Times Magazine had an article about the turmoil at Lehman Brothers, a Wall Street investment banking house. A rough-edged Mr. Inside, Lew Glucksman, succeeded in driving out their Mr. Outside, Pete Peterson, and within a year this proud, hundred-year-old firm was swallowed up by Shearson.

Glucksman thought he and other inside types could do it all. He found out otherwise.

I have a stockbroker friend who uses a formula for investing that's based on the Mr. Inside/Mr. Outside rule. Whenever a company goes public for the first time, the underwriter usually holds an informational meeting. They take place in fairly elegant surroundings, so that as the niceties are observed, the stockbrokers can be subjected to the pitch from the company's executives that will induce them to go out and peddle the stock to their customers.

'Usually the pitch for the stock is made by the company's Mr. Outside,' says the stockbroker, 'but if there's no Mr. Inside up there at the speaker's table, wearing a brown suit with sleeves two inches too short, I pass on the deal. The same if the shrimp on the buffet table are as big as your fist and the Scotch is the really good stuff, 'cause that means there's no product there. No manager that's worth anything or has any clout would let the company buy Johnny Walker Black for a bunch of stockbrokers.' He says it hasn't failed him yet.

I'm not a Mr. Inside. I can't do it all, but it took a long time for my ego to accept that. When I did, I went out and hired a key man to run my plant and made him the president of the company. He does a much better job of it than I ever could. But conversely, I'm a better salesman than he is.

There's another side benefit to dividing the inside and outside roles.

LESSON 40

Never be your own hatchet man

Ike had Nixon; Reagan had Regan; every ball club has the manager of the moment. You have to get someone who can make the tough, mean, unpopular decisions – and can take the fall when they get too tough, mean, and unpopular. You are the peerless leader. You couldn't really *know* what a meanie old Frogface is or you wouldn't let him treat people that way. Of course you know. That's why you hired him. If you're out there on a shoeshine and a smile, serving on community boards, making new business presentations, being quoted in the paper on the future of the widget industry, you don't want to be known around town as the guy who lays off employees at Christmas, dislikes labor unions, and shortens the coffee breaks. Your public performance won't fly if you're the one who has to crack the whip at home.

How do you run a business? You understand the strengths and weaknesses of the people you're dealing with and exploit them – in the best sense of the word – to build strong personal loyalties and to make sure everyone plays his or her proper role. Even though that sounds like a bad B-school text, doesn't it make a little more sense?

LESSON 41

On the other hand, if you are going to be your own hatchet man . . .

Be a damn good hatchet man.

Some managers were just made to play the heavy. Classic slave drivers like Harold Geneen, Lyndon Johnson, General George Patton, and Vince Lombardi ('He treated us all alike, like dogs') are too larger-than-life to be prettied up by public relations.

No large organization – especially one with a strong desire to be a winner – survives without a little bit of Attila at the top. Often it's the COO or the director of operations. Occasionally it's the CEO himself. When that happens, the CEO inevitably pays a price – with the community and the press, with his employees – but, most of all, with his counterparts in other companies.

If you are determined to be a tough guy, wisdom says you better bring these strengths to the fore:

- exceptional intelligence with the ability to ask tough questions from 9:00 A.M. until quitting time, whenever that is.
- fair-mindedness (you might call it the ability to hit with either a left jab or a right cross)
- maintenance of extremely high performance standards for yourself·
- commitment to keep your guard up continually (and cynically)
- the ability to shed criticism like a duck shedding raindrops

In other words, you must have the mind-set of a drill sergeant. Your troops aren't going to love you, but they'll respect you — as long as you can prove to them you're tougher than they are and you're willing to drive yourself even harder than you're driving them. Establishing this kind of style is like playing corporate 'King of the Mountain'. Everybody competes with everyone else in the place for turf or gets thrown off the pile.

The emotional investment for this kind of 'persona' is enormous, and not much is left over for all the other things a CEO must be in the 1990s to win trust and initiate change. It's not my first recommendation, but if it's you — go to it.

LESSON 42

Little things don't mean a lot; they mean everything

Vince Lombardi said, 'Victory doesn't mean a lot. It means everything.' What victory consists of *is* everything. Doing everything right. The point is, a successful business is like a successful football team: You don't have to be winners; just make fewer mistakes than your opponents.

If you run a business, there are 1,001 ways to screw up every day, and almost all of them can be avoided with a little more attention to detail or common courtesy. A customer calls and gets put on hold for too long or gets shuffled around to three or four different people. Goodbye, customer. The order got lost or is late or is the wrong color . . . or whatever. Hello, Chapter 11. I don't have to tell you what can go wrong. *Everything* can go wrong. If you're in charge, your job is to minimize the mistakes.

You can't be everywhere at once.

You can't get away with, 'it's on the truck' or 'it's in the mail' for very long.

You know better than to try to solve your problems by merely sending out another memo.

Yet you still have to try to impress all of your people with the importance of paying attention to details.

How do you accomplish this?

The strategy is leadership.

Nobody is going to believe it's important unless you, the boss, make it seem important. The tactic you use is by example.

Here are a couple of ways in which I've seen it done.

Lou Holtz, the head football coach at Notre Dame, is a stickler for detail. He does it this way:

The team has a road game at Purdue. They've been instructed to wear coats and ties to the stadium because they'll be closely observed as representatives of the University of Notre Dame. They're waiting to board the bus to go to the stadium for the game. And waiting. Coach Holtz shows up. Doesn't say a word. Just goes down the line and looks them over. And over. Finally he goes up to one of the players, smiles, reaches up and straightens the player's tie, and then nods to the driver of the bus. Not until then is the door to the bus opened and the team permitted to load up.

He hasn't said anything, but the message is as clear as if he tattooed it across the center's fanny: If you're going to be a winner, guys, look like a winner. Little things mean everything.

Bud Grant, another great football coach and motivator, had another gimmick. The very first drill at the very first practice session of every Viking training camp was the same: Grant personally demonstrated and the players practiced how to line up properly for the playing of the national anthem. And they got the message: Let the other teams stand around like they're in a bread line; you're special, you're winners, so you look and act like winners every second you're part of this team.

You can preach about little things and discipline until your tongue hangs out, but it won't work unless *you* yourself find a way to dramatize it and make it seem important enough so the message gets through.

What's the difference between the CEO of Company X prowling the halls and looking for messy desks and Holtz straightening neckties or Grant showing grown men how to stand up straight? After all, they're all tidying up with the same objective in mind: to demonstrate leadership and instill a sense of the importance of detail. What the coaches understand is that no matter what the lesson is, you can teach it only by instilling a sense of pride, not shame in the pupil. Poking into offices that are, presumably, not on public display, says, 'You don't know how to do your job.' Shaping up public appearances says, 'Let the whole world see you look as good as you are.'

A master of driving home a large point by making an issue over a small one is Carl Pohlad, who owns the Minnesota Twins baseball team, a piece of the Minnesota Vikings, and is on the *Forbes* 400 list of the super rich. Pohlad made his fortune in banking and soft-drink bottling.

During a luncheon negotiation with Pohlad involving a major real-estate undertaking, the young tiger on the opposite side of the deal was asked by the waiter what he'd like to drink.

'I'll have a Coke,' he said.

'No, you won't,' said Pohlad. 'You'll have a Pepsi.'

Needless to say, Pohlad's soft-drink plants bottled Pepsi-Cola. More important, his mild indignation, though seemingly lighthearted, gave him just the tiny edge he needed to score a few extra points in the negotiations.

Another multimillionaire in the beverage business, Jay Phillips, who owns the Phillips liquor interests, made his point about the proper brand to serve in a slightly different but equally direct fashion. Upon arriving as a guest in the home of a business associate, Phillips would eye the liquor cabinet to see what was being served. Smart hosts always saw to it that Phillips labels were displayed.

You may not be the nation's largest Pepsi bottler or a Jay Phillips, but if you've filled out the Mackay 66 and know your target, you'll not only avoid costly gaffes . . . you'll also be able to use the little things to score big.

LESSON 43

How to spot a winner

General William Westmoreland was once reviewing a platoon of paratroopers in Vietnam. As he went down the line, he asked them a question: 'How do you like jumping, son?' 'Love it, sir!' was the first answer. 'How do you like jumping?' he asked the next. 'The greatest experience in my life, sir!' exclaimed the paratrooper. 'How do you like jumping?' he asked the third. 'I hate it, sir, ' he replied. 'Then why do you do it?' 'Because I want to be around guys who love to jump.'

Dennis Connor, the man who put the blocks to Australia and won back the America's Cup in four straight races, explained in a few words how he did it: 'I surround myself with quality people that make me look good.' Winners also know how to bounce back after a hard hit. Connor's crewman John Grant put it this way: 'Dennis likes to know he has people who will make the right moves when things go wrong.' And that's the right management instinct if you're at the helm of a twelve-meter yacht or a billion-dollar business.

Winners surround themselves with other winners. A winner knows he's a winner. He doesn't need second-raters and yes-men around to feed his ego. He knows he'll win more, and go farther, with associates who not only can keep up with him but who also are capable of teaching him something.

If you're about to form a new business connection, whether it's a job or a joint venture, don't just look at your opposite number. Look at his subordinates. Does he trust them? Does he delegate to them? Do they complement his talents by being strong managers while he's an entrepreneur? Or are they just his clones? If they're weak, you have a problem. You'll not only have your hands full getting anything done your way, you'll also be completely dependent on your new associate's personal capabilities and energy. There won't be quality staff backup. Not a good situation in which to find yourself.

LESSON 44

Your best people may spend their most productive time staring at the wall

There's a story going the rounds that a manager who couldn't use his concert tickets for Schubert's Unfinished Symphony gave them to his work study management executive – in nonjargon, the efficiency expert – and received the following report after the performance:

1. For considerable periods, the four oboe players had nothing to do. Their number should be reduced, and their work spread over the whole orchestra.

2. Forty violins were playing identical notes. This seems unnecessary duplication, and this section should be drastically cut. If a larger volume of sound is required, this could be achieved through an electronic amplifier.

3. Much effort was absorbed in the playing of demi/semi-quavers. This seems an excessive refinement, and it is recommended that all notes be rounded to the nearest semi-quaver. If this were done, it should be possible to use trainees and lower-grade operators.

4. No useful purpose is served by repeating with horns the passage that has already been handled by the strings. If all

such redundant passages were eliminated, the concert could be reduced to twenty minutes. If Schubert had attended to these matters, he probably would have been able to finish his symphony after all.

Efficiency achieved at the expense of creativity is counterproductive. Don't equate activity with efficiency. You are paying your key people to see the big picture. Don't let them get bogged down in a lot of meaningless meetings and paper shuffling. Announce a Friday afternoon off once in a while. Cancel a Monday morning meeting or two. Tell the cast of characters you'd like them to spend the same amount of time normally spent preparing for and attending the meeting at their desks, simply thinking about an original idea. And it has to be something they've never mentioned before. Don't even require them to submit the results. Just see what happens.

If you discover one of your executives looking at the wall, like the oboe player, instead of filling out a report, go over and congratulate him or her.

They are probably doing the company a lot more good than anything else they could be doing. They're thinking. It's the hardest, most valuable task any person performs. It's what helped get you where *you* are. THINK: It's the one-word motto of the most imitated company in the country, IBM. Don't stifle it. Encourage it.

LESSON 45

It's more fun when it's spontaneous

No, I'm not talking about sex again, though the same principle applies. Have you ever noticed a certain lack of enthusiasm for what passes for fun of the usual corporate variety?

You don't have to wait until the calendar tells you it's time for the Christmas party or the office picnic or some other form of compulsory fun.

When you sense that the pressure has really risen and stayed on too long, when you can feel the concentration level going down – that's the time to have the party or to come up with tickets to the ball game or the concert. You'll be pleasantly surprised at the results the next morning after that freebie from the boss. You noticed what was happening: You cared – and you did something about it.

LESSON 46

Have you ever seen a stand-up strike?

I know that a lot of people are tired of hearing about 'how they do it in Japan.' But I had an experience there just a couple of years ago that you deserve to hear about. It illustrates to me how employees can care. It also says that managers must take employees seriously when employees express their views and feelings.

I was invited to visit the Komatsu Corporation factory in Osaka. The company is one of the world's largest and most efficient manufacturers of heavy equipment. Sales are $9.5 billion annually.

Just before the plant tour was scheduled, I got a call in my hotel room. Some of the workers were on strike. Did I still want to see the plant? Sure. Why not? We take the tour. We pass a group of workers wearing black armbands, moving around doing their jobs. 'Who died?' I asked. 'No one,' they told me. 'These are the people who are on strike. They strike by wearing black armbands, the traditional Western symbol of bereavement, while they continue working. They're sad that things have come to such a sorry state of affairs that they are in disagreement with management, but such things do sometimes happen. So they are on strike – by wearing black armbands.'

But the plant keeps operating. No production is lost. The workers keep on earning wages. They keep talking with management about the problems. And they keep on working!

And, by the way, they keep on slamming us into the pavement with the quality, efficiency, and value of the products they are producing in direct competition with us.

The lesson here is about creativity, not just productivity. The Japanese have found a way for the plant to stay operational and for the workers both to keep drawing a paycheck and to keep their grievance alive and visible to their managers every minute of the workday.

The payoff was that the terms of settlement of the grievance probably weren't much different from what they would have been had the workers shut down the place. All they missed was the chance to shout insults at each other across the bargaining table for a few months.

LESSON 47

It isn't practice that makes perfect; you have to add one word: it's perfect practice that makes perfect

Lombardi again, but let me try to put a new wrinkle on it. You can practice all day long, but if you don't really know what you're doing, no matter how much talent you have, you're only perfecting an error.

Look at the great athletes and musicians. There are no walk-ons at the Super Bowl or Carnegie Hall . . . or in corporate boardrooms, for that matter. The level of performance in those exalted places is only partially a reflection of talent. There are two other qualities that are indispensable in making it to the top: expert coaching and iron determination. Let's start with coaching. Only we'll call it teaching.

You're reading this book for a reason: in the hope that buried somewhere in these pages are at least one or two ideas you'll be able to use to make a buck. For the short time you, the reader, and I, the writer, have to spend together, I'm your coach. We both know that no book is going to change your life. Only you can actually change your life. I can't do it for you. No teacher can.

A teacher is not there just to acquaint you with the tools of your trade; a teacher *is* a tool of your trade, no matter what that trade is. You never stop needing teachers. The great musicians never stop taking lessons, never stop trying to improve. Arthur Rubinstein used to say that if he missed a day of practice, he noticed it in the quality of his performance. If he missed two days, the critics noticed. And if he missed three days, the audience noticed.

Whatever it is you do, you can be better at it if you just keep on learning. I certainly have not mastered the art of making envelopes, selling envelopes, or developing new envelopes.

The minute I persuade myself that I have, that I have learned all there is to learn about the subject and can relax, that's the moment my competition will find a way to do any or all of the above better than I can and will hand me my head. The annals of business are filled with stories of companies that thought they had it made and could milk their enterprises as cash cows without having to bother about improving their products or service. It's amazing how fast they found their markets disappearing.

Forbes described a classic example recently: Howard Johnson's. I grew up in an era when Howard Johnson's had the fast-food business pretty much to themselves. But instead of plowing enough of their profits back into research . . . developing new markets . . . anticipating trends in consumer attitudes . . . Howard Johnson's stopped learning and laid back thinking they had it made. They found out that they didn't

You can apply that lesson to your own business. Hire people who are still learning, people who feel that learning is a lifelong process, either in the classroom, the office, or at home. Encourage your employees to learn by paying their tuition for them. Develop a business library and stock it with written materials and video and audio cassettes. Show them you want them to grow – and your business will grow, too.

LESSON 48

Trust the experts . . . to be wrong

There are two types of experts, and it's very important to be able to distinguish between them: There is the expert who can make something happen, and there is the expert who can tell you what he or she *thinks* is going to happen. Get all the advice you can afford from the experts in category one, but be very, very cautious about the category-two types.

Let me give you an example: One of my best friends was the president of a very distinguished regional brokerage house, and as such had more than a rooting interest in the economic outlook. The firm paid a sizable retainer to a prominent economist who provided them each month with short- and long-range economic forecasts. It was beautifully written, filled with clever quotes and closely reasoned arguments . . . and always wrong. Nothing unusual there, as it has been said of economists that they are the only professionals who can make an excellent living without ever being right in their entire careers.

My friend knew all this, of course, but he was afraid to cancel the arrangement because of fear he might someday miss a major turn in the economy. He hedged his bets, though. When he had to make a really serious decision – a major underwriting, for example – he also used the economic forecast feature in *Fortune* magazine – which he bought at the newsstand every other week – and got better results.

Whether it's economists, the most prestigious of the

professional pundits, or stock-market forecasters, or political analysts, or just plain old sports handicappers and racetrack touts, my advice is the same: Be extremely leery. Rely on these people to tell you why something *happened*, but don't rely on them to tell you why something is *going to happen*. They don't know any more than you do – and neither do their computers. When it comes to forecasting events with a large number of highly volatile variables, any one of which could determine the outcome, experts are less than expert. Trust yourself and your gut, and you're likely to do at least as well.

LESSON 49

It isn't the people you fire who make your life miserable, it's the people you don't

When I use this line in speeches, I get more 'Amens' than a Billy Graham sermon.

You can't put a little plaque with those words on your desk, but if you are a manager, you would be well advised to engrave them on your psyche.

LESSON 50

The best way to chew someone out

There isn't any. But you do have to do it, so you may have
to master a technique that both suits your style and the
occasion. The Ken Blanchard one-minute-in-hell method is
hard for me. If I'm really on a tear, I'm not ready to stop
after a minute. And I don't.

Nothing works all the time, but there's one method I've
saved for the biggies. I sit in my big, comfortable office. I
reach out for the culprit through my secretary, who gives
him a 'little tip . . . I've never seen Mr. Mackay so angry.' I
make him stew in the anteroom for up to half an hour.
Okay; so far, nothing you haven't done a few times
yourself. The purpose of the preliminaries is obviously to
make him focus on his mistake and be painfully aware of
the depth of my wrath.

He is summoned in. He stands in front of my desk. I
speak. 'Jack,' I say, rising up, scowling, and pointing to my
chair, 'please go over and sit in that chair.' He sits in my
chair. I sit in what would normally be his chair. 'All right,
Jack, now what would you say if you were me?'

Oh, how they hate that chair. I once overheard a
conversation where they were talking about me and one
fellow said to another, 'Did he give you the *chair*?' You'd
think it was Sing Sing! It's unfamiliar territory, so that
generates discomfort automatically. Second, because of
what is coming down, they know they don't *belong* in the

133

position of authority represented by the boss's chair, and that makes for an added burden of guilt. Believe me, four out of five times they were harder on themselves than I ever would have been ... though, of course, no one has ever fired himself. Because I don't do the chewing out myself, no never-to-be-forgotten-always-to-be-resented phrases are lodged forever in their memories. They do all the dirty work.

But it's not surefire. One fellow out of five I tried it on was very flip about it. So I had to wait until the next time ... and I did not give up my chair when I fired him.

LESSON 51

Never let anyone, particularly a superstar, pick his or her own successor

Every manager should insert a small addition to his prayers each night in which he invokes the aid of a Higher Power in ensuring that his predecessor is always an incompetent. In fact, there's no better situation for a manager to inherit than following an incompetent. Obviously there's nowhere to go but up. A more subtle variation on the theme occurs when a superstar is about to leave. Since he did such a spectacular job, it seems logical to ask him to share just one last bit of his superior wisdom: Mr. Superstar, who should be your successor? Whoever he recommends, smile sweetly, and cross that name off your list.

It's just bubble gum psychoanalysis, but I believe that, consciously or unconsciously, no one really wants his or her successor to succeed. They recommend candidates likely to fail, thereby making their own achievements all the more remarkable.

Back in the 1970s, Bill Fitch, the current Houston Rockets' coach, was a giant success in restoring Minnesota basketball to national prominence. After building up the program, he decided to go on to greener pastures. The assistant coach, with Fitch's *strong* recommendation, got the job . . . and was gone in a year. The other leading

135

candidate for the job – the fellow who got turned down – wound up at Indiana. That was Bob Knight.

The same thing happened a couple of years ago when Bud Grant, head coach of the Minnesota Vikings, retired the first time and persuaded the Vikings' management to hire assistant coach Les Steckel. Steckel was totally wrong for the job and, after the Vikings suffered a 3-13 season, Grant was back again, hailed as the savior of the franchise.

The weak predecessor / strong leader / weak successor syndrome isn't confined to sports. Andrew Jackson's hand-picked successor as president of the United States, Martin Van Buren, was a dud. One of the persistent myths of American history is that a dying Franklin D. Roosevelt passed over ex-Secretary of State, ex-U.S. Supreme Justice Jimmy Byrnes for vice-president in 1944 because he saw the hidden quality of greatness in Harry S Truman. Roosevelt picked Truman precisely because he seemed to be such a perfect hack. Roosevelt would have been astonished, and no doubt dismayed, if he had known how well his successor performed.

Anyone who thinks he or she is indispensable should stick a finger into a bowl of water and notice the hole it leaves when it's pulled out.

LESSON 52

Give more conventions and you can give fewer raises

All successful sales organizations offer a constant round of morale-booster meetings, incentives, awards and recognition. No matter how often salespeople are told 'It isn't personal' when they're turned down, professional sales managers realize how psychologically draining those rejections are. It's a never-ending struggle to keep their people up and motivated. What applies to salespeople also applies to the rest of the work force. Everyone needs to feel appreciated.

Most businesses aren't very glamorous. Envelopes may turn *me* on, but to most people in the endlessly exciting envelope game, it's just a job. If you want to goose up the morale a little bit among your middle managers, give them some unexpected recognition. For most people, bragging rights are just as important as money.

Send a few key people to a convention or a seminar or two. Give it the full treatment. Call them in unexpectedly, tell them the company hasn't had that great a year but you want to recognize their superior performance by sending them to such-and-such a school/seminar/convention. If you're ready to give the person even more of a boost, throw in a ticket for the wife or husband. They're to report back on what they've learned, of course, but make it clear you really selected them because they are just the sort of person

137

you want representing the company, and you want to reward them for it. Then send out a memo announcing exactly what you just told them, or put it in the house organ.

You've accomplished several things: You've told your people you notice and appreciate good work, and you've created a performance incentive without locking yourself into a costly and ever-escalating program. That, of course, is all in addition to your existing recognition and awards program.

LESSON 53

How many salespeople do you have?

When people ask me that, I tell them we have 350. 'Wow!' they answer. 'How many employees do you have?' 'Three hundred fifty,' I say.

As I mentioned before, we manufacture a common, ordinary kind of product that's been around in similar form for hundreds of years. Nobody stops me on the street and says, 'Gee, what a great envelope you guys make.' The truth is, in our industry everybody makes pretty much the same product line and the pricing is very competitive.

Our success depends on marketing. There's no magic formula for making every employee aware of the importance of marketing to our company. It's a daily grind. Our strategy is to create awareness among our people. We use devices like one we started years ago. The parking space closest to the door of our main office has a sign: 'Reserved for [you fill in the name] Salesperson of the Month.' The key to that parking lot gimmick isn't just recognition to an individual. It's also that the parking space is closer to the door than *my* parking space or anyone else's. It's a very specific way of saying that sales are the key to our business.

There are two very simple signs I want to tell you about. You won't find them at the novelty shop or the cutesy sign store, because I made them up myself. One hangs on the door to my office. When the door is closed, you come eyeball-to-eyeball with it. It says, 'If you know where you can get us some business, come in.' The second sign is on the little round table in the conference area of my office. It says, 'Our meeting will not be interrupted ... unless a customer calls.'

LESSON 54

Get bored easily

Professional managers can repeat the same task over and over, but most successful entrepreneurs can't handle boredom. The difference in these two familiar types runs so deeply that, if you're a manager, it's unlikely you'll succeed in the role of entrepreneur, just as entrepreneurs tend not to make very good managers. There's a place in the world for each. The message here is to entrepreneurs.

McKinsey & Company did a study of the members of the American Business Conference, which grew 20 percent per year over the five-year period prior to the publication of the report. There is one common thread running through these operations: The people who run them tend to be entrepreneurs who just can't stand corporate bureaucracy, organization charts, and manuals for operating procedures.

Entrepreneurs share a common trait with good salespeople: Both are able to communicate a sense of self-confidence and importance about their mission that is contagious to all around them.

Entrepreneurs scratch before they itch. They dare to fix things before they break because it is part of their makeup to seek out fresh challenges.

They determine the agenda; they set the pace; they dominate the field of play. Pit an entrepreneur against a manager, and the entrepreneur is constantly forcing the manager to abandon his own plans and react to the entrepreneur's initiative.

If you're an entrepreneur, you know it. And if you are, your competitors have reason to dread it when you feel the onset of restlessness. It means you're ready to make another move. Don't fight it – it's the entrepreneur's greatest strength. At the same time, recognize your greatest weakness: an eye for detail, which all too often translates into an inability to manage the financial end of the business.

If you're an entrepreneur, be frank enough about your own limitations to get yourself a George Wilson to handle the day-to-day operations. Twenty years ago, when Wilson was stewing over whether to take on the commitment of moving the Billy Graham offices to a newer building, he called Graham and asked his advice. 'I don't call you and ask you what I should preach,' said Billy. 'Don't call me about what you should do with buildings.'

LESSON 55

Ask an old grizzly

The ability to listen to others is not, typically, the entrepreneur's greatest strength.

If you're the oldest guy in the shop, if you're the one others turn to when they want to hear about the 'old days,' it's time to find *yourself* an even older grizzly.

When I first bought Mackay Envelope, I was twenty-five. My lawyer, the one I hired after I fired the young hotshot who told me not to buy the envelope company, was sixty. My accountant was fifty-eight, and my banker would admit to being seventy, but I think he was closer to eighty. They didn't know a thing about the envelope business, but they didn't need to. They had seen enough business problems in their lifetimes to be able to deal with anything imaginable without knowing the ins and outs of my particular industry.

Though everything that happened to me in my first five years of business was new to me, nothing was new to them. And even when I didn't take their advice – and often I didn't – they were a calming and reassuring influence. And that's something every businessperson, novice or experienced, has need of from time to time.

I'm a bit past twenty-five now and getting closer to old-timer status myself, but if I learned anything from those old-timers, it was that I didn't have to shoulder the whole load alone. There are a lot of qualified advisers out there to help . . . if we only ask them. Try it sometime. Thinking of adding a new product line? Considering relocating your plant? Afraid to take a strike, but feel in your gut you should? Making an acquisition? You're not the first person who's had to wrestle with those problems. Ask an old grizzly. You may have to listen more than you talk, but that won't hurt you either.

Knowing when not to work hard is as important as knowing when to

'I'm a great believer in luck,' said Stephen Leacock, the Canadian humorist, 'and the harder I work, the luckier I get.'

The founder of Holiday Inns, Kemmons Wilson, never got his high-school diploma, but they asked him back anyway to give the commencement address to a graduating class at the school he attended. He said, 'I really don't know why I'm here. I never got a degree, and I've only worked half days my entire life. I guess my advice to you is to do the same. Work half days every day. And it doesn't matter which half . . . the first twelve hours or the second twelve hours.'

Curt Carlson, chief executive of the privately held Carlson Companies, which includes the Radisson Hotels, the world's largest travel agency, and the Country Kitchens restaurant chain, started selling premium stamps out of the trunk of his car and ended up with one of the nation's great fortunes. *Forbes* magazine estimated his wealth at $500 million. He has a very simple philosophy about work. He says the first five days of the week, Monday through Friday, are when you work to keep up with the competition. It's on Saturdays and Sundays that you get ahead of them.

A lot of people would call Carlson a workaholic. Of

145

course, he doesn't think so; to him, work isn't work. Obviously, he doesn't work for money only. As you might imagine, Curt is a pretty bright guy and undoubtedly realizes that anyone with $10 million can be just as happy as someone with $500 million. For Curt, *making*, not *having*, the extra $490 million was fun. Playing golf is work. (Guess what he's better at.)

But you and I don't have to be workaholics to be wildly successful.

Ken Blanchard, the coauthor of *The One Minute Manager*, has it right. It's the 'peak performers' who do the best job of handling the load. They can turn on tremendous bursts of speed for a week, two weeks, three weeks, when it's needed for some particularly important task, and then be unashamedly lazy in between when the nature of the work is routine.

Peak performers can distinguish between goal-oriented performance, really productive work, and mere wheel-spinning. They are astute in avoiding the latter. Classic entrepreneurial boredom sets in . . . and then they get the hell out of the way for a while.

So, yes, you have to be able to work very, very hard, but no, you don't have to approach every assignment in typical 'Type A' full-speed-ahead fashion. Knowing when to throttle down can contribute as much to your performance, and your life-span, as knowing when to throttle up.

Curt Carlson and Kemmons Wilson are a special breed; they never stop working. But most of us would probably improve our own performance if we did take off more often.

I don't take many *real* vacations, and I also get away from it all by being involved in activities around town that get me out of the office routine – or at least I tell myself I'm getting away from it all. But then, I'm the kind who could be just as happy with the $10 million as Curt is with his $500 mill.

LESSON 57

Owning 1 percent of something is worth more than managing 100 percent of anything

I have a confession to make: If I had written this book ten years ago, the heading here would have suggested the exact opposite, something like TAKE IN LAUNDRY BEFORE YOU TAKE IN PARTNERS.

If there's any characteristic that distinguishes the entrepreneurial type, it is a half-mad fanaticism about going it alone, without anyone poking a nose into his business, asking questions, or telling him what to do. Nothing is tougher for an entrepreneur than letting go of total control.

Well, the world has changed. Every business, even as elementary a human pursuit as making envelopes, a product that is essentially no different from what it was 150 years ago, is becoming more complex because of the introduction of sophisticated machinery, marketing, and financing techniques.

The seat-of-the-pants entrepreneur, no matter how talented or intuitive, needs professional skills he can never hope to master himself. He will have to buy those skills in a marketplace where the sellers have also become much more sophisticated about the value of their abilities and how to charge for them.

Time for another cautionary tale.

An entrepreneur friend of mine holds controlling interest in a professional sports franchise. It has been very successful, in large part because the entrepreneur had the vision to see that television was upgrading his market from a small, local audience to a vast, nationwide one. And also because he was smart enough to hire the best nuts-and-bolts man in the business to run the franchise.

One day, the nuts-and-bolts man came upstairs and asked for a piece of the action. Not a particularly large piece. In fact, even 1 percent would have been adequate to satisfy his hunger for security and prestige, the need to feel he was an owner and not a mere hired hand.

But the entrepreneur, the man with Space Age marketing vision, also had Stone Age labor relations attitudes. He refused. The manager left.

Our entrepreneur didn't realize that any business relationship in which one party has an obvious edge over the other won't be to the advantage of either because it won't last. Although the franchise hasn't exactly fallen on hard times – it's next to impossible to lose money in that game – the entrepreneur has clearly lost his touch.

The next manager he hired turned out to be even more demanding and a shrewder corporate politician. Now the entrepreneur is trying to keep from being thrown out of his own business entirely.

I wonder if he ever thinks back about that meeting of years ago, when, if he had only been willing to give up just 1 percent of his franchise, he never would have faced the prospect of losing it all.

These days, if you expect to keep your business, you'll need professional skills to run it, and the people who have those skills are likely to be just as aware of their value as you are.

They expect a piece of the action. You're going to have to give it to them or risk losing them, and possibly something much more important.

LESSON 58

Dig your well before you're thirsty

When I saw how effectively Bill Jacobs was running Mackay Envelope, I didn't wait for him to cross the hall and ask. I offered him a stake in the business, and one that was considerably larger than 1 percent. Since then, several of my major competitors have taken a run at him, but he's not leaving. He's an owner now.

Should I have waited until I had to make the offer?

Not unless you think it's smarter to buy when everyone else is bidding than when you see value long before it's recognized in the marketplace.

LESSON 59

Treat your own people the way you treat your customers

The salesperson's classic tactic of knowing as much as possible about the customer begins with learning names and progresses to using tools like the Mackay 66. Now let's see how the entrepreneur can expand that concept. Again, I'll illustrate with a story.

A politician is the ultimate entrepreneur. He is out there all by himself, with no corporate identity to hide behind. Politics, at least in the pre-Watergate era, was the last of the freebooting, swashbuckling, no-holds-barred, nineteenth-century businesses, where competitors slugged it out toe-to-toe, winner-take-all.

A professional politician is someone who has mastered both the tools of persuasion and the rough-and-tumble tricks of the marketplace. Anyone who makes it to the top in politics can usually make it anywhere.

I met Hubert Humphrey for the first time when I was fresh out of college. I'd hit the books pretty hard for four years, but I spent a lot of time hitting golf balls, too, and got to be a pretty fair collegiate player. I tried to persuade my father that destiny beckoned me to the pro circuit.

My father countered by setting up a series of meetings for me with various big shots he knew. I think the idea was that they were to talk me out of taking up golf and try to convince me to do something constructive. The reason he

150

thought it would work was that I was always kind of a hero-worshiper, and these people were all well known, the kind that my dad wrote about every day in the papers.

Humphrey was first on the list. I went into his office, he bounded out of his chair Humphrey-style to greet me and said, 'I hear you're a great golfer, Harvey. I envy you. I wish I had that talent. Just keep at it, and maybe someday' — he jerked his head over in the direction of the White House, where Ike the golfer was practicing putts on the rug in the Oval Office — 'you'll get to be president, too.' I was amazed. Instead of boring, well-meaning advice, which is what I eventually got from everyone else on the list, what I got from Humphrey was the hand of friendship no matter *what* I decided.

Humphrey knew I wasn't going to listen to a word he said about what I should do with my life. I'd make up my own mind about that. Rather than viewing me as a chore to be disposed of as soon as possible, or an object of his oratory, Humphrey saw me for what I really was: a customer, a soon-to-be-voter. He used the few minutes we had together to achieve his objectives. He made me his friend, and, of course, I became a supporter and contributor to his campaigns.

As entrepreneurs, we like to think of ourselves as far-sighted, but we're seldom as farsighted as a Humphrey. Instead of thinking of our employees as customers to be won over to achieve our long-term objectives, we think of them as automatons, pieces of machinery who are summoned to carry out our short-term objectives. It doesn't work that way. Take the trouble to do what Humphrey did. Do your homework. Find out enough about the people you're working with so you can show some genuine personal concern about them. Express that concern and make them your friends. One at a time. Your long-term success depends on their performance. To a greater extent than you may realize, they're performing for you, for your approval, not just for your paycheck. If you can make them believe that your approval means something, by taking a personal interest in them you will have taken a major step toward securing your own long-term success.

Successful politicians realize they get most of their votes retail, one at a time, from constituent service and personal contact, not wholesale, from their positions on the issues. In other words, a voter will often support someone he disagrees with, but never someone he dislikes. It works the same way in business.

A little-known journalist friend of mine once interviewed Jeno Palucci, the entrepreneur who built up and then sold two major food businesses for a reported $100 million. The interview took place in the dead of winter in a fancy hotel suite with Palucci surrounded by aides. When they finished, Palucci got up, went over to the closet, got out the writer's coat, and then everyone stood around while the five-foot, five-inch, $100 millionaire Palucci struggled to get the impoverished writer into his Sears, Roebuck overcoat. Just a tiny, little thing, but to that writer, Palucci defined himself by that one courteous gesture.

'I've been eating Jeno's Pizza Rolls for the past ten years,' he said, 'even after Jeno sold the company. I sure wished I liked them better.'

LESSON 60

How to be fired

Those of you who follow baseball will recall that owner George Steinbrenner fired Billy Martin five times as manager of the New York Yankees. After one of the stormier episodes, Steinbrenner hired Yogi Berra to replace Martin. One of the sport's more inventive historians tells the story that Berra was rummaging around in the desk in the manager's office when he found two envelopes that had been left behind by Martin. There was a '#1' on one and a '#2' on the other. Both were sealed and addressed 'To my successor,' and below that, the words 'Open only in case of emergency.' Berra put them back in the drawer.

Berra started out with a very good won-lost record. Suddenly the road got a little bumpy, the Yankees lost a few, Steinbrenner went on the warpath, and Berra rushed to the office and opened up envelope #1. Inside was a single sheet of paper. On it was written 'Blame it all on me.'

Terrific! That's exactly what Berra did. The team got back in the winning column and Steinbrenner got off his back. Four weeks later, another losing streak. Steinbrenner went berserk. Berra ran back to the office and opened up envelope #2. It said, 'Prepare two envelopes.'

Next to losing a loved one, losing a job can be the most traumatic experience many of us face in a lifetime. But if you are one of those who have worked for someone who is impossible to please or are in one of the notoriously high-turnover businesses, you should be preparing two envelopes every day: the 'I stay' envelope and the 'I leave' envelope.

Survivors have their 'I leave' envelope cleaned, oiled, and ready to fire when that road does get bumpy. They don't panic if they're terminated. They use the occasion of their firing to extract the maximum amount of concessions from their employers . . . employers always feel somewhat guilty about letting go even the most incompetent employee. Survivors network extensively within their industry and their community for a new position long before the ax falls.

Be honest with yourself. You can probably tell if you're about to be let go. If you are, anticipate. Getting fired could be the best thing that ever happened to you. It won't seem that way at the time. When Churchill was turned out as prime minister after leading Great Britain through the darkest hours of its history, his wife tried to comfort him by telling him it was a 'blessing in disguise.' 'If it is,' said Churchill, 'then it is very effectively disguised.' But Mrs Churchill had a point. After all, look what happened to Ronald Reagan after Warner Brothers released him. Or Lee Iacocca after he got fired by Henry Ford.

LESSON 61

You can't solve a problem unless you first admit you have one

Alcoholics Anonymous has used that principle as a starting point to reclaim thousands and thousands of lives. Thousands more are never reclaimed because it's so *hard* to change.

Sheer stubbornness has destroyed a lot more bottom lines than new technologies. There were just as many mean-spirited jibes at Coca-Cola for abandoning its original formulas as there were at Ford when it unveiled the Edsel. The difference was that Ford decided it was going to prove the marketplace was wrong and stuck with its mistake far too long. Coca-Cola realized early that while humiliation was inescapable, horrendous losses need not be. It cut its losses, and its mistake cost it a lot less money than stubborn pride cost Ford.

One thing professional stock and commodity traders learn early is that they don't give away medals for courage in the marketplace. There is only one reward the marketplace has to offer: money.

If you're not making any, bail out. Quickly.

LESSON 62

If you can afford to buy your way out of a problem, you haven't got a problem

Facing the results of a huge mistake, many people will stop dead in their tracks, too emotionally drained to see that any problem that can be solved with a checkbook isn't really a problem, it's just an expense. Once the mistake is recognized, what's lost is lost. Don't freeze. Act. If you can buy your way back on the right track, do it. Quickly.

Then it's no longer a problem, it's just a negotiation over the cost of the solution. Here are a few examples.

1. Bud Grant, Minnesota Vikings coach, decides to get out before he burns out. His successor proves to be less than successful, and four thousand season-ticketholders threaten to cancel. Solution: Buy your way out. If they want Grant, get them Grant. The man who took the Vikings to four Super Bowls is reluctant, so management makes that famous offer, the one you can't refuse. Grant comes back, and the cancellations stop. Grant cost them plenty, but leaving a running sore untreated would have cost them a hell of a lot more.

2. A key customer is furious because your factory blew the delivery date. Solution: Buy your way out. Tell him, *no charge* for the shipment, even if it means you have to hand out

$5,000 to $10,000 to $25,000 worth of merchandise. You will keep that customer forever, and your firm's reputation and morale are preserved. Sure, it can cost big money, but which is cheaper: eating the loss, or trying to put a new key customer on the books and having a once key customer spread poison all over town?

3. One of my best customers and I were at Lake Placid for the 1980 Winter Olympics to see the hockey finals between the Soviet Union and the United States, which happened to be the main event that year. I was told we had good seats – I paid a fortune for them – but when we got to them, we were behind an obstruction and so high up you could get a nosebleed. The customer was unhappy; I was embarrassed. Even though it wasn't my fault, did I let him sit there brooding about the miserable time he was having in my company? No. Solution: Ben Franklin came to the rescue. I went to the main floor, spotted two high-school kids, and asked them if they were interested in switching seats for $100. They thought I was nuts, smiled, said yes, and they were happy. I was happy, my customer was happy. And the United States won the game.

LESSON 63

'I have never seen a bad résumé': John Y. Brown

The former governor of Kentucky's wry observation should be tattooed on every manager's forehead. Everybody's a winner on paper. It's in the flesh that the differences stand out. Who would have hired failed haberdasher Harry S. Truman based on a résumé, or chosen 73-year-old Dixon College graduate Ronald Reagan over Walter Mondale, a polished lawyer, after comparing their paper credentials? Hiring the right people is the greatest talent a manager can have because good people produce good work and lousy people do lousy work. That's why Alfred Sloan, the manager who made General Motors, spent so much time hiring people even for positions that seemed routine. It's why at the prestigious firm of Latham and Watkins – as business consultant David Maister has written – "all candidates get twenty-five to thirty interviews, compared to a norm in the legal profession of approximately five to ten interviews.' And Latham and Watkins is regarded in knowledgeable circles as one of the best run law firms in America. I try to take it a step farther. I get involved in the hiring process not just to get good new people but also to remind the ones who are already with us about what's important at Mackay Envelope.

Every few years we have to hire a new receptionist/ switchboard operator. Now, ordinarily this is a job that would be handled routinely by a company's personnel department, and not even by the head of the department.

Not at my shop. I do this one myself. And I make it the biggest deal since the search for a replacement for Johnny Carson. Employees are asked to submit candidates and reminded that for ninety-nine out of a hundred people who come into contact with Mackay Envelope, the first significant impression of the company is from the receptionist/switchboard operator.

By the time we find the right person, everyone in the place is part of the program and totally aware that courtesy and attention to detail are critical concerns at Mackay Envelope and that you're someone special if you're asked to work here. We're not filling slots; we're looking for capable, caring, conscientious people.

As a result, when you call Mackay Envelope, your call is usually answered after no more than three rings; you hear a pleasant voice, a voice with a smile in it; and if you've called us more than once, chances are the receptionist recognizes your voice and calls you by name before you even have a chance to identify yourself.

Just recently we ran an ad for a salesperson and received 135 résumés. Thirty were screened through initial interviewing, and I interviewed the eight finalists – and rejected all of them. We were back to square one again.

Searches for our firm may take thirty days to two years. 'But how can that be? How can you tolerate unfilled vacancies for that long?' I've been asked. First, we plan our needs so we aren't backed up to the wall when any one person leaves. Second, I've been in business twenty-seven years and I've been 'open for hiring' fifty-two weeks a year for twenty-seven years. When anyone really solid comes through the door, they have a job – even if we don't have a place. That gives us bench strength. Third, our selection process is so rigorous that our long-term retention rate is well above 80 percent. Getting hired by Mackay Envelope is like a battlefield commission. It generates pride for the recruit and for the entire work force – which sees real evidence that management is doing its job.

If you want to understand the fundamentals of hiring, go back to the basics of buying and selling. You, the employer, are buying and he or she, the candidate, is selling. The résumé, the interview, letters of recommendation, references – these are all selling tools. Put yourself in the candidate's shoes: Do you expect the suit he's wearing are his best duds or tomorrow's Salvation Army contribution? Are Mary's handpicked references going to tell you she is a genius or a dunderhead? What do you expect the reference letter to say: 'I hope your company can do something with Jack because – God knows – we certainly couldn't!'?

Now, should you be offended or distrustful because the candidate is selling hard? Not on your life! Selling skills may be exactly what you're looking for. But there is a big difference between admiring a beautifully produced television ad and believing it. When you hire, it's your job to be the product quality engineer who tests and stamps approval. You know: 'Inspector #12 – they can't be Hanes until I say they're Hanes.'

I'm not going to go into the techniques of interviewing a candidate. Much has been written on that by specialists elsewhere. At Mackay Envelope we have a ten-step hiring process that I *do* think is unique and useful. Sure, we don't use all ten steps for every new hire, but we use more of them than you might think. If it sounds as slow and as painful as the Chinese water torture, imagine *your pain* at the other end if you have to fire someone you mistakenly hired. Then the investment doesn't look so bad.

1. *The candidate is invited over for an interview.* Nothing exceptional here, except that our personnel interviewer is a skilled gatekeeper, bright enough to know what management is looking for and secure enough not to automatically screen out intimidating or unusual candidates.

2. *The candidate is invited back for six to eight follow-up interviews with members of our management.* Again not unusual, except that the interviewers discuss their findings and make a

160

specific hire/reject recommendation with reasons why. (It's great training.)

3. *I talk with them for thirty minutes.* Or rather, *they* talk with *me* for thirty minutes. I can't tell you how many job interviews occur where the CEO prattles on about how he built the company or his views as an industry statesman while the candidate is graded on how sympathetically he nods his approval.

4. *I talk with them on the phone for thirty minutes.* How much of your business in and outside an organization is conducted these days by telephone? Can the person project, persuade, and communicate clearly over the phone? Now is the time to find out if you're hiring Phil Donahue or an answering machine.

5. *I dial up some outside sources.* Check out the candidate in the industry. Who knows or should know about this person? Contact people you trust and who have a good feel for other people.

6. *I interview candidates in their home setting with their spouse and children.* I want to see the candidate's personal values at work in the most revealing setting. It's also a great integrity test. Does the candidate's home life match the description in the interview?

7. *I socialize with the candidate in a different environment.* Is the candidate a classical music or movie buff? Then it's off to the concert hall or the theater with candidate and spouse. How does this person act in a social setting? It's especially important for salespeople because that's when they need to be their most skillful and persuasive.

8. *The candidate sees two or three of my peers in other, noncompetitive companies in my town.* The visits are brief. How do I get my associates to devote time to this? Of course, I reciprocate and review *their* final candidates!

9. *A trip to the Master.* Every city has a master of profession – master controller, master purchasing agent, master executive secretary. The successful candidate has to pass muster with the master. I make a point of personally knowing the masters. (By the way, their leads are often a terrific way to find candidates in the first place.)

10. *A trip to the counselor.* The industrial psychologist's analysis is often enlightening but never binding. It is usually most helpful in addressing someone's strengths or weaknesses after you hire them.

Those are the ten steps to successful hiring: Mackay's Boot Camp for Natural Selection. By the way, I never call their references. In the middle of the interview, I always ask for the name of an influential teacher or mentor who knows their strengths and weaknesses intimately. It's surprising how often that name differs from the ones on the résumé.

Happy hunting! And remember, don't bag it unless you expect to be happy with it hanging in your office for some time to come.

LESSON 64

The acid test for hiring

Ask yourself, How would you feel having this same person working for your competition instead of for you?

LESSON 65

If you want to be Santa Claus, your sled better be able to pull a trailer

When I started in business in 1960, I thought it would be a nice gesture if I gave my employees a little Christmas bonus. Money was out of the question, so I gave each one of them a Christmas turkey. The first year I gave away twelve turkeys; the second year, it was thirty-five; then fifty, then seventy-five, and now it's 350 . . . and there is no way I'll ever be able to quit without having a revolution on my hands. There's nothing the matter with being generous, but beware of spontaneous gestures unless you remember they have a way of becoming permanent 'traditions'.

LESSON 66

What's the best way to save time?

Spend more time on time management. You're in as good a position to save time as your richest and most powerful competitors. Over a lifetime, it's incredible how much time you can save, and the advantages you can achieve, while you're sitting on your duff in your car. For example:

1. Put a phone in your car.
2. Always phone ahead when you make a call on a customer or prospect.
3. Always park your car in a getaway position.
4. Use the car's cassette deck to listen to tapes that teach you something, instead of tuning in the usual babble on the radio.
5. Never travel without a tape recorder at your side so you can "write notes" to yourself while you're driving.

Add a few noncar time-savers to that list:

6. Drop that tape recorder into your coat pocket and keep it by your bedside. You've now doubled the number of hours you can be getting ahead of your competition.
7. Always carry something useful to read.
8. Never go to the bank during the Friday lunch hour.
9. Never have coffee with another salesperson, only with a customer.
10. Just for the hell of it, for an entire week, substitute reading a business publication for the time you spend reading the sports page or the variety section.

LESSON 67

Don't get mad and don't get even either

Like everyone else, I have accumulated my share of enemies in the course of a lifetime. It's nothing to be ashamed of. Forgive thy enemies is very difficult advice for many of us to follow. After all, if someone has harmed us, we tend to want to get back at them. We can carry our grudges for many, many years.

And, of course, it is totally counterproductive. I once fired an employee who then went into competition with me and began using what I felt were unfair business tactics. The psychic energy and accumulated bitterness that went into my thoughts of revenge consumed me for the better part of five years.

It was more than a waste of time, because whenever I thought about it, I grew vindictive and sour, and those attitudes spilled over into everything I touched. As a result I lost more than did the object of my revenge.

If you can't take the best advice and forgive your enemies, then take the second best and forget them. The only way you can achieve true revenge is not to let your enemies cause you to self-destruct.

LESSON 68

Know thine enemy

Knowing your competition is just as important as knowing your customer.

Let me illustrate the point by calling forth a brief tale of high intrigue and the clash of arms from chronicles of the envelope game.

A manufacturer I know has a major competitor, with a larger and more modern facility, located directly across the street from his own plant. They're both fine companies, and for years my friend was rankled by the fact that his competitor was the sole supplier to one of the area's *Fortune* 500/NYSE-listed companies. Though he was always willing to accept the proposition that no account was locked up forever, he couldn't dislodge the competition and crack this prospect. He tried all the standard ploys. And he got nowhere.

Then he decided to try a different approach, and instead of concentrating on the customer he focused on his competition. Did they have a weakness that played to one of his strengths?

It turned out they did. The prospect had expanded operations in the South. When he analyzed the competition, he realized that their closest plant was in New York. He had a plant in Birmingham, Alabama. Did he use that information to gain a competitive edge? You can bet your last #10 envelope he did. It was obvious that his competitor couldn't match him in price or service in that particular area.

The next time one of my friend's reps walked into the prospect's office, he was able to offer a package for the southern operation that gave him his first major inroads into the account and left his competitor in the dust.

He never would have won the account if he had kept his attention solely on his prospect. His unwillingness to believe his competitor was invincible led him to develop sufficient knowledge of his competitor's operations to cause him to seize the initiative and close the sale.

Unless you have a unique product or service, or run a state-owned bakery in the Soviet Union, competition is a fact of life. You must deal with it. The best way is to gather what knowledge you can and then act.

Along with everything else that has changed, the old gladiatorial style of competing has passed. No longer do we just climb into the ring and have it out. When Flavius thrust his broadsword, Spartacus raised his shield. That was *reactive* competition, based entirely on waiting for the industry leader to move, and then countering. The outcome depended upon the strength, speed, weaponry, and reflexes of the combatants – and whether the Coliseum was muddy or not on the day in question.

Planning was minimal. In marketing, this old routine translated into minding the four P's:

- Product
- Price
- Place
- Promotion

It worked or it didn't. That day. If it didn't work, you tried another prospect.

Today we compete differently. Warfare, in both the military and corporate modes, has become much more sophisticated, more analytical, more strategic rather than just tactical. We corporate types, with our management teams, the general staffs of our boardroom bunkers, press the noiseless buttons of our computerized war machines to create:

- Marketing strategies
- Position papers
- Long-range plans
- Niches, goals, objectives
- And more information than we can possibly digest

The oversimplifications of the gladiatorial era have been replaced with the overcomplications of the era of technology. Now, we literally study our competitors to death. It has become impossible to stay on top of all the data and still run a business.

Many managers, while calling for more information, are overwhelmed by the information they already have, and what they do have, they use piecemeal or improperly. Knowledge is *not* power unless it is used. It does not have to be perfect, but it does have to be accessible. And it requires managers who have the judgment to act on it properly.

At Mackay Envelope, we put this idea into practice not too long ago. Conceptually it's a spin-off of our customer profile, so we call it our competitive profile. It's here in its entirety on the following pages. And we fill it out on every significant competitor we have.

MACKAY ENVELOPE CORPORATION
12 'P'S COMPETITIVE PROFILE

Date _____

Last updated _____

By _____

1. Pedigree

Name of company _____

Headquarters location _____

Subsidiary or independent? _____

If subsidiary, of whom? _____

_____

Publicly/privately held _____

2. Physical Scale

Number of plants _____

Plant locations _____

Number of employees _____

What geographic areas can they serve best? _____

What geographic areas can they serve adequately? _____

3. Performance as an Investment

Fiscal year ends on what date? _____

Last year's revenues _____

Last year's profits _____

Performance trend past two to three years _____

Any unusual financial issues (heavy inventories, etc.)? _____

_____

D&B rating _____

Overall financial condition (check one): Strong _____

Satisfactory _____ Shaky _____

4. Pricing

Their pricing attitude (check one): High and mighty _____

Down and dirty _____

How do they respond to pricing competition? _____

_____

5. People

Unionized (if so, by whom)? _____

Who are the two to three most important players in the firm
and what are their positions? _____

What is their reputation as an employer? _____

_____

6. Positioning
What is their target market? _____

What unique products (features) do they offer? _____

What is this firm's short-term strategy? _____

What is this firm's long-term strategy? _____

7. Plans
Do they want to hold position/grow aggressively? _____

Are they targeting an acquisition/rumored as an acquisition/ merger candidate? _____

_____

Are they rumored to be developing any products or services?

_____

8. Performance as a Supplier
Average delivery time _____

Quality of service _____

Service strengths _____

Service weaknesses _____

Hard/easy to resolve customer problems _____

With what accounts do they have the best relationship? _____

_____

What accounts would it hurt them the most to lose? _____

_____

What is their practice regarding entertainment, gifts, etc.? ____

_____

Who are <u>their</u> most important suppliers? _____

_____

Their business practices reputation (check one): Fully above-board _____

Less than perfect _____

9. Prestige in the Business Community
Characterize their reputation overall _____

_____

Has this firm (or its principals) had any legal or image problems? _____

Does the firm (or its parent) have any strong charitable, social, or civic involvements? _____

How about top management of the company? _____

How is the company regarded within our industry? _____

By our trade associations? _____

10. Probing for Data

Do we have any employees recently recruited from them who should be debriefed? _____

What customers either used this competitor in the past or use them in conjunction with us who are reliable information sources about this firm? _____

Who else do you know who can supply information about this company? _____

Do we know how this company perceives us? (lazy, aggressive, technically superior, etc.) _____

Any recent articles in the trade press? Financial or general press? (If yes, make sure copies are placed in the file.) _____

11. Prize Fight . . . Them and Us

Which accounts do they have that we want? _____
_____

Who is their salesperson(s) for these accounts? _____
_____

What piece of the business (territory, market segment, etc.) do they operate in? How can we profitably grow our share?
_____
_____
_____

Have we (or anyone else) ever won business from these people before? If yes, how was it done? _____

12. Post mortem

We will beat this competitor if we do the following five things right:

A. _____
_____

B. _____

_____

C. _____

_____

D. _____

_____

E. _____

_____

Note what this is not. It is not a bound book, or a five-inch-thick computer printout. It is not fancy. But that's the point. Fancy does not get read or used. This does.

Now let's see how to compile this and how to use it.

When we launched this program, we set aside about half a day a week to fill these out. It took us two and a half months to complete all the questionnaires. Don't let that intimidate you. A lot of the data can be gathered by staff and assistants. For the meatiest parts, three or four of us would sit down as a group: my marketing and sales head, the relevant sales manager, the salesperson, and me.

Now's let go through the questions, step by step:

1. Name and location are obvious. You want to know if you're sparring with a sub or an independent and how much power is behind them.

2. This profile is designed for manufacturing, but it can be easily adapted for businesses that deal with the consumer. In the envelope business, geography is very important to costs and service quality. If you're selling semiconductors, though, you may want to rephrase the question and ask which market segments or industries you can serve well or acceptably.

3. You would never step into a boxing ring without knowing if your opponent was healthy or just over the flu; it affects how you plan your fight. And it isn't just _you_ who needs to know, it's also the salesman and the account manager. After all, who decides to throw the left hooks on a daily basis?

4. Get to know your competitor's moves on pricing, and watch out for changes. This is one area where companies often switch their dance step.

5. Unionization means loss of flexibility. Know who the real decision-makers are, and make sure *your* personnel director knows, too. A firm with morale problems is usually a choice target for aggressive competition.

6. Who and what are they aimed at? Read their sales promotion material and their annual reports. Today's trends to disclosure have made many businesses strategic 'open books'. Periodically test the water: Are they really achieving the strategy they say they are pursuing?

7. 'Stay tuned for further developments.' With today's merger mania, anything can happen to a competitor. The sale of the business can mean dismemberment *or* a huge infusion of fresh resources.

8. Know how your opponents do business. That doesn't just mean prices and products. What is their service record? How do *they* treat *their* resources, and who are they? When the client goes out to lunch, is it lobster mousse or chicken wings? Know their ethics. You don't have to stoop to conquer, but know what you're dealing with. (In areas like this, make damn sure you know your facts, and keep your files locked.)

9. Reputation and civic involvement are critical. If two firms do business principally because their respective presidents sit on the same symphony board, you better find a way to deal with that.

10. Some of the most valuable data are soft: opinion and word of mouth. Filter such information cautiously, but use it by all means. Intelligence gathering doesn't mean conducting a Watergate; it means nurturing trusted resources and reading the trade press. Make sure the sources are confidentially

documented for future use in the event your salesperson or marketing head takes a walk in pursuit of greener pastures.

11. Now, what direct gains do we want to make against these opponents? Look at the game film: How were they beaten before?

12. What's your action plan? Be brief and direct. Don't forget to come back in three to six months to see if you're doing what you said you would – or if some new actions are in order.

By this time you probably have figured out an astounding feature of this questionnaire. It is not just what it tells you about your competition that makes it so valuable, but what it tells you about your own strategy.

Once you have compiled a stack of these questionnaires, sorted them out, compared them, and categorized them, you'll start to see a pattern emerge from step 12. The actions you need to take to make competitive inroads will repeat themselves. Your competitive profile has become a strategic plan. I don't know of a better, simpler, more effective, or more usable method of developing one.

LESSON 69

Don't be intimidated by a reputation

Von Clausewitz, the great military strategist, observed that it is the mark of inadequate commanders to fail to seize the initiative because they overestimate the strength of their opponents. For years, General Motors and IBM dominated their industries despite critical deficiencies. The companies that should have been willing to fight them for market share really weren't competitors, just symbionts, looking for unfilled market niches where they could pick up a few crumbs that fell off the master's table.

When the competition finally came, it came from people across a cultural chasm so wide they didn't understand what it was that made these giant companies so wonderful, or from shoestring operators who had nothing to lose by ignoring the popular mythology.

It took the Japanese to show us how vulnerable GM was – and a handful of gutsy American entrepreneurs to do the same to IBM – and now both companies are being forced to earn their livings on the basis of performance. They didn't think they had to concern themselves with the competition. They do now. And so should the rest of us.

Chapter V

QUICKIES

◆

QUICKIE 1

Gratitude is the least deeply felt of all human emotions

You've heard it expressed before, both in the vernacular ('What have you done for me lately?') and in the classical modes ('How sharper than a serpent's tooth it is to have a thankless child'), but it still bears repeating: Don't expect gratitude to last any longer than it takes for the recipients to say they're eternally grateful.

We arrived where we are today because a number of people gave us a leg up along the way, but ask for a show of hands and 99.9 percent of us consider ourselves self-made men and women.

Hatred and even love endure, but there is in the human makeup that which is unwilling to bear the burden of being grateful, and therefore morally beholden, to anyone for very long. So whatever you do for your kids, your spouse, your subordinates, your boss, or your friends, just remember: You'll be a lot happier if you think of it as doing it for yourself. And then try like hell to forget you did it, because the beneficiary has.

QUICKIE 2

It's not your last good idea

I believe that there's a rational explanation why new ideas tend to spring up from unrelated sources almost simultaneously. At any given moment, there are certain widely accepted goals . . . say, getting rich, or having thin thighs. With all kinds of people in all kinds of places building on and using the same body of knowledge and common experience to tell you how to reach those goals, you're bound to find some marked similarities between the routes.

It seems to happen all the time with scientific discoveries. So why not with creative ones, too? In fact, we're such prisoners of our times and own environments that a trained eye familiar with the tiny stylistic quirks peculiar to each period can easily detect most art fakes . . . and tell you exactly when they were created. We think alike more often than we'd like to admit. And if you've got one good idea, it's a pretty good indication that you can come up with another.

I've done it — especially when I thought someone had stolen my idea. And so can you. You've got to have more than one good idea. Once is not enough. (With apologies to the late Jacqueline Susann.)

◆

QUICKIE 3

Buy cheap cars and expensive houses

I suppose there are people with real money who drive Cadillacs and Mercedes. I don't know many. As long as practically anyone can own one of these so-called prestige cars, who's going to be impressed? In fact, the opposite is true. If you can afford a fancy car, you make more of an impact driving an ordinary one. If you're a big, fat guy, then buy a big, fat Olds 98 but not a Caddie. Don Dayton, whose name is on the door of every Dayton Hudson store, drives a Chevrolet. Okay, so it's a new one every year, and because it's the only one I've seen since 1942 that's jet black with white sidewalls, it does stand out a bit. Still, it's a Chevy.

If there ever was a expensive purchase where reverse snobbery was called for, it would be buying a car. Cars depreciate. Houses appreciate. And, by the way, Don Dayton has never lived in a Chevy-style house.

QUICKIE 4

How to get to know a celebrity

You and I may be fascinated by meeting celebrities, but for the most part they're bored by meeting us. When you meet a celebrity, what can you talk about that *they* will remember and give *you* some real take-home value?

Talk about whatever it is they do that made them famous, and you can see their eyes glaze over as they give

179

the same responses they've given ten thousand times before.

The trick is to avoid the fan syndrome and treat them like human beings. Find where *their* interests lie. You can bet it isn't talking about what they do for a living. (Does your doctor like to talk shop at cocktail parties?)

My wife, Carol Ann, is a master at this. We once met O. J. Simpson at a party, and before long they discovered that they were both Art Nouveau lamp enthusiasts. That's right: Mr. Macho Football Player collects table lamps. And loves to talk about his collection.

Now, if you are into collecting celebrity heads as trophies to trot out at dinner parties, isn't it a lot more interesting to be able to reveal that you compared notes with O.J. on the outrageous prices they're getting for Tiffany lamps than to recite some shopworn story about a long-forgotten half-back option?

Years ago I was in the first delegation of businessmen to visit Cuba after Castro had taken power. I was given a one-on-one with Castro. I spoke in English; Castro, who supposedly spoke no English, spoke in Spanish. An interpreter translated.

I managed to find his hot button immediately. '*Comandante*, I noticed that you are in excellent physical condition. How do you do it?' I asked. The library had loaned me a biography where I'd read that before he got into politics, he was given a tryout as a pitcher by the old Griffith-owned Washington Senators.

His eyes lit up . . . *before* the translation. 'Bowling,' he said in Spanish, and he went on to describe how he had installed a bowling alley in the basement of the Palace of the Revolution. Then he reached into a breast pocket and pulled out a little notebook. That was where he kept a running tally of his scores and the results of his matches with his generals. The final column showed who owed what to whom. Unsurprisingly, they *all* owed Castro; he had beaten every one of them. 'What an amazing coincidence,' I said. 'I happen to have won the University of Minnesota bowling championship three years in a row.' 'Oh, you did?' Castro blurted out – in English. All pretense of his inability to speak English had vanished in the excitement of having discovered a fellow bowler.

In an instant he realized what he had done, and the conversation concluded quickly. Still, I've been dining out on the strength of that story for years, and I learned a lot more about Fidel Castro than I would have if we had simply gone a few rounds of the standard capitalism vs. communism exchange.

The key to finding out what you need to know is the most useful book I have in my office: *Who's Who in America*. Who's in it? It seems damn near everybody is, that's who. A while ago I was asked to speak on a program that featured Art Buchwald. The event was built around him, so not only did we have Buchwald as a speaker before a mass audience, but he was also our guest at dinner, where I was seated next to him.

Okay, what do you talk to Art Buchwald about? Well, to answer that, you go to *Who's Who in America*. It turned out Buchwald was in the Marines. Nothing there for me. But he also graduated from the University of Southern California. Now, there was a place where I had some contacts. So instead of fumbling around trying to find some common ground or staring at the tablecloth for two hours, there it was, the right button to turn on Mr. Buchwald's lights from the start. Some people you run into can't be found in *Who's Who in America*. In those cases, your friendly local librarian will steer you in the right direction.

QUICKIE 5

The best r&d firm in the world is never more than a phone call away

You're not always going to be where you have a *Who's Who in America* at your fingertips.

You can only pester your stockbroker so much for company reports before he starts to expect to take it out in trade.

And unless you have an excellent 'in' at the local paper, you'll never have access to their morgue – the prime source of information on local people and events.

But for the price of a phone call you do have a marvelous research facility at your command.

The public library.

Want to know the names of the officers of any publicly held company?

Their product line?

Latest earnings?

Want to get any congressional vote? The status of any piece of federal legislation? The winner of the 1944 World Series? (the St. Louis Cardinals over the St. Louis Browns, four games to two in the 'Streetcar Series').

Don't send your secretary on a wild goose chase or hire a lawyer to get the answer.

Call the main branch of your public library. They'll tell you over the phone.

Some of the most distinguished people in this country make their livings in the nation's public libraries, particularly the New York Public Library. In fact, they have their offices there – in little lock-up cubicles set aside for their private use.

They're authors.

Every day they go down to the library, mine the raw ore they find in the stacks, and convert it into the modern novels and nonfiction we read every day.

One of the reasons so many major authors live in New York is the quality of that library.

If those writers can make a living out of it, you can use it to your advantage just as effectively.

QUICKIE 6

'Nothing is greater to one than one's self is' — Walt Whitman

The next time someone calls you a one-way, egotistical son-of-a-bitch, don't forget to thank them. They have just provided a strong endorsement of your mental health. 'Self-esteem' is a buzz word these days, and it's about time. The higher it is, the better you get along with yourself, with others, and the more you'll accomplish.

Humility is the most overrated of human emotions. The two worst failings, many of us were taught when we were young, were lying and bragging. I'd rather stick with Will Rogers, who said, 'If you done it, it ain't bragging.'

What's the matter with being proud of what we have done or think we can do? In my opinion, humility is what our parents and teachers try to stuff us with when we're six years old to make us easier to handle, but it's unnatural. When we're young, we're full of the sense that we can and should be able to do almost anything.

Dr. Anthony Greenwald, a psychologist at Ohio State University sees the 'egocentricity bias' – the reinterpretation of events to put ourselves in a favorable light and the belief we have more control over events than we actually do – as a sign of mental well-being.

That makes perfect sense to me. Dr. Greenwald can call it the 'egocentricity bias,' but I call it optimism. And I call optimism a quality that consistently delivers results. Did you ever get a good performance out of a pessimist? (By the way, no one ever called himself a pessimist. Pessimists always call themselves realists.)

Optimism involves self-delusion, a belief that our own abilities are superior to the obstacles that logically should overcome us. But that's exactly what's needed to perform any heavy-duty assignment.

How can you be any good unless you think you can accomplish what you're not supposed to be able to accomplish? Top performers in athletics or business are always convinced they can be heroes, even if they don't shout it from the rooftops. And it shows. In fact, baseball scouts call that look 'the good face,' the sense of self-confidence that radiates from winners.

Don't let the 'egocentricity bias'/optimism be snuffed out in you. It's a hell of a lot more productive than humility.

QUICKIE 7

There is no such thing as a bad memory

Little Johnny, in sixth grade, came home with a report card that was all D's and F's. His father asked why. 'I can never remember anything,' answered Johnny.

The old man said, 'Well, you're not going to any more baseball games until you get your grades up. And to begin with, forget tonight's game.'

'Now, wait a minute,' said the kid. 'You can't do that to me. The Dodgers are in town. Valenzuela is pitching. He was 21-11 last year with a 3.14 earned-run average, led the league in complete games and victories and was second in innings pitched with 269 and strikeouts with 242.'

Can't remember?

You can remember anything . . . if you're interested in it. A man I know can't remember the name of the secretary of state, but he remembers the lyrics to every song Irving Berlin ever wrote. Let me add that Einstein couldn't remember his own phone number. 'Why should I bother,' he said, 'when I can look it up?' The things he did remember, nobody could look up unless Einstein himself wrote them down.

Nobody expects you to always remember the names of your customer's kids, but that doesn't mean you can't have them dancing right off the end of your tongue when you need them – if you use the Mackay 66.

You write them down *immediately* after you leave your meeting with your customer. They go straight onto the form. Five minutes before you walk into his office the next time, you review that form and you're a genius . . . or at least you appear to be.

Don't try to rely on your memory for stuff like that. Pale ink is better than the most retentive memory. Use the Einstein approach. He was no dummy. If it's written down, you can look it up. Just be damn sure you write it down.

QUICKIE 8

Put your memory where your mouth is

We all know people from modest circumstances who have made it big. And flaunt it. The newly rich often demonstrate their insecurity by adopting an ostentatious lifestyle. It's their way of proving to themselves and the world that they've become very important people.

Our economic system encourages a certain amount of that. How else would we sell Porsches and BMW's to guys who could walk to work? Swimming pools to people who don't like to swim.

But financial success can create a more serious mind-bender: a tendency to forget the people who helped us get started, to use those newfound riches to distance ourselves as far as possible from our origins.

Nobody who started with nothing and ended with something got there all by himself. Once, long ago, someone saw a quality in *you* that made them want to give you a leg up. Would they feel the same way about you today? Be honest. If they wouldn't, if success has changed you, then it's time you got back to your roots. Whatever material things you have now could vanish just as quickly as they came. Better hold on to the one asset you started with – the appeal that caused other people to trust and believe in you. Stay in touch with your mentors. If you let yourself lose contact with them, chances are you're also losing contact with what got you where you are.

QUICKIE 9

Stay sharp by predicting the future

Play this game with yourself: Predict the outcome of events that interest you.

The stock market
Elections
Athletic events
Whatever

There are three rules to the game. One, you have to write your predictions down (otherwise, you'll cheat, you devil). Two, you also have to write down the *reasons* for your predictions. Three, when you lose, you have to force yourself to analyze *why* you lost, why your reasons didn't hold up.

If your ego needs an occasional cold shower, this little exercise will provide you with a lifetime supply. It will also force you to reexamine and adjust your reasoning without having to pay any penalty for being wrong. You'll find that the more you do this, the more accurate you'll become. And if you find you have a real talent for it, then, but not until then, you should back that talent with cash.

QUICKIE 10

It usually pays to look good, but sometimes it pays a lot more to look bad

A Minneapolis businessman was on vacation in Waikiki over Christmas. He went to the beach for hours every day and acquired an immaculate tan – from the neck down. Not a ray of sunshine reached his face, which he kept totally shaded by a hat, sunrise to sunset. His friends were curious, of course, but too embarrassed to ask him why, figuring that he might have medical problems that kept him from exposing his face to the sun. Finally an acquaintance asked him. The businessman laughed and said, 'Who, me? A skin problem? Hell, no. Next week I have to testify before the state legislature and I'm asking them for a huge subsidy, and I wouldn't dare be caught with a tan on my face.'

QUICKIE 11

Take a millionaire to lunch

Earlier I told you how important it is to use short notes to make that personal gesture to your employees and customers, and how that simple device has become almost a trademark of some of the most savvy businesspeople I know. Let me add a tailgate to that advice: Put the most important people you know on that list of people to whom you drop notes. Yes, it's lonely at the top, and the bigger they are, the more strokes they need,

One of the forces that drives a superachiever far harder than the rest of us is an inordinate need for recognition and approval. Money is one way to measure it. That's why they work so hard to get it. But so is a compliment from a friend. And those are a lot harder to come by. So if you know one of these types, let them know you appreciate them.

I have a buddy who does it a little differently than I do. He has founded the 'Take a Millionaire to Lunch Club'. 'If you want a surefire way to tell whether or not a guy is rich,' he says, 'it's when the check comes. The more bucks they've got, the less they have to prove they've got, and the easier it is to beat them to the punch when the bill comes.'

QUICKIE 12

It's not only who you know, but how you get to know them

I once took a class at UCLA that included the topic, 'Eighteen Reasons Why You Should Travel First Class'. I thought the title was a come-on for whatever the prof *really* wanted to talk about, but it wasn't.

The bottom line and prioritized first reason was the people you meet. There is camaraderie in the first-class section that you won't find in tourist. I said camaraderie, not snob appeal. When you're in first class, everyone wants to know why everyone else is willing to pay an outrageous 20 to 30 percent premium for the privilege of drinking warm, sweet champagne and disembarking twenty seconds ahead of the rest of the passengers. As a result, particularly on a long, international flight, you do get to know your fellow fliers and can develop some valuable contacts. I have.

QUICKIE 13

To a normal person, $10 million will seem like enough

'But anyone who thinks that's enough is not the type who can acquire that much in the first place.' – James K. Glassman, magazine publisher.

QUICKIE 14

How to beat the law of supply and demand

A general manager of a major sports franchise told me this story. One year, after the team finished way below expectations, hundreds of people canceled their season tickets. Team management realized that if the public was aware of it, the cancellations could snowball. So they kept the news confidential, didn't panic, and developed a remarkable strategy to fill those empty seats.

In the local paper they ran a $10 blind ad that read, 'Leaving town. Four season tickets for sale.' The response was overwhelming. When they filled those orders, they ran another, similar ad, and quietly parceled out those tickets. Ultimately they managed to sell all the canceled season tickets without anyone ever knowing what was going on.

Some friends in New York told me the same principle is used in their restaurant business. When they open a new restaurant, for the first two months they tell about half the people who phone in for reservations that the place is full for whatever night they request and to please phone back.

Obviously, what they're doing is what the sports organization did, maintaining the illusion of demand regardless of supply. The lesson here is not that people are sheep but that in a capitalist economy, everything that is sold is a commodity, whether it's stocks, hard assets, season tickets, or restaurant seats. No one wants it if it's too easy to get; if they can't get it, if it's in demand, then everyone wants it.

Marketing hasn't changed since we described it in Lesson 1: Our sense of the worth of an object is not derived from its intrinsic value but from the demand that has been created for that object.

QUICKIE 15

There is a place in the world for anyone in the world who says, 'I'll take care of it'

The meeting is just about over. The boss has handed out the assignment. You're about to troop out the door and back to the cubicle down the hall to do whatever it is that's supposed to be done.

Two things are happening at that moment: You're trying to figure out how in the world you're going to do whatever impossible, tedious, harebrained job you've just been handed, and your boss is waiting to hear you say the magic words. So be smart. The first thing you have to satisfy is the boss's need, not yours.

Forget about how you're going to do it. Since you're going to have to take care of it – that's what you're getting paid for – why not let him hear what he wants to hear: 'I'll take care of it.'

Babe Ruth got paid to hit home runs, and of course, he did, 714 of them, but the most memorable one he ever hit was when he 'called his shot' and pointed to center field with his bat before he hit it there.

Call your shot. Saying you're going to do it before you do it, counts. It counts big. You've given your boss peace of mind. You're someone who delivers. Can you think of a better reputation to have in any business situation?

QUICKIE 16

Never give the same speech once

There's an anecdote in a recent book by David Halberstam, *The Reckoning*, in which he describes how Philip Caldwell, then president of Ford Motor Company, was so maddeningly demanding that he required the services of ten different speechwriters to prepare the same speech.

I'd be willing to bet an envelope or two that once Caldwell was finally satisfied with the written result, he delivered it to his target audience without having tried it out on a similar audience beforehand.

It makes no sense to put in all that work getting a speech written without getting a firm fix on the whole point of the exercise: audience reaction.

There's a reason Broadway shows don't open on Broadway. They open out of town because it gives the company a chance to gauge the effects of their material on an audience. These pros know that there is simply no way to know what works and what doesn't by reading the lines to themselves. You have to have that crucible of live reaction.

If you give speeches, doesn't it make sense to do what you do with every other major product your company produces: Do some market research? Take the show on the road – not in front of your PR people, but disinterested types far removed from your company, like a local service club, the Rotary, or Kiwanis. Try out those corny jokes, hone that material . . . until you're positive you've got a winner. It will not only improve the text, it will also improve your own performance, because you'll have confidence that what you are saying will generate the right response.

Most successful people are good on their feet. We're an information society, so the ability to transmit that information in an intelligent, succinct, and persuasive manner is about as valuable a skill as anyone can possess. 'Brilliant but inarticulate,' may be a description that would apply to a nuclear physicist but not to any head honcho corporate types I know. They're brilliant *and* articulate. I once knew a fellow who bounced around from one profession to another over the years, from law to politics to selling securities to publishing to advertising to writing. Not just six different jobs. Six different professions. He wasn't exactly at the top of the heap, but he still managed a nice living.

'How do you manage to jump from one thing to another like that?' I asked him, as much out of envy as curiosity, since I have never ventured far from the envelope game.

'I haven't,' he said. 'I've always done the same thing. Sell words. The job descriptions are just a little different. Cops have a name for it. They call us "word dinks."'

Learn to use the language. Written and spoken. Anyone who's a word dink has got it made.

QUICKIE 17

There are two times in life when you're totally alone: just before you die and just before you make a speech

Those lines are from a poster advertising Vander Zanden, Inc., a company that teaches the fine art of speechmaking to business executives. When I first saw the ad, I signed up for the course. Then I began to sign up my employees. What I realized is what most successful speakers already know: You may be totally alone when you're making the speech, but you don't have to be alone when you're *preparing* for it.

When you speak before civic and professional groups, you and your company gain public recognition and credibility. It will help your business, but that's not the only reason you should do it. The real reason is that the skills we learn by overcoming our terror of standing up in public and spilling our guts carry over into the rest of our lives. We gain self-confidence and assertiveness, which allow us to be better managers, better salespeople, and better leaders.

A speech is a sales call. It's the toughest kind of call you can make: You're selling an intangible, an idea, not a product. And it's a cold call on fifty or a hundred closed minds, many of them complete strangers who have no reason to believe a word you're saying.

But just as you never have to make a cold sales call, there

are no cold speaking calls if you do your homework. The solution is another wrinkle to the Mackay 66, which I call '11 Ways to Win Your Audience'.

No two audiences are alike. But if you can answer these eleven questions, you'll be able to tailor your material to the interests and concerns of each group, and I guarantee you'll win them over.

The alternative is found in another Vander Zanden, Inc., slogan: 'If you doubt the concept of eternity, make a five-minute speech.'

11 WAYS TO WIN YOUR AUDIENCE

1. Why did this group invite me to speak? (stated reason)
   How was my talk publicized and positioned for this audience?

2. What is this group's purpose?

3. What are the chief characteristics of this group? (professional, social, demographics, career level, etc.)

4. Who spoke to the group recently?
   How were they received?
   Can I get copies of their remarks?

5. Who were the speakers who addressed this group most successfully in recent history?
   What made them successful?

6. How can I personalize the speech for this group?
   What humor will work?
   What is a 'no-no'?

7. Who are the opinion leaders in this group?
   Which of them will be there?
   How do I reach them?

8. Who will introduce me?
   How will he or she position me?
   What nice things can I say about him or her?

9. Will I be expected to answer questions?
   What are the key questions I can anticipate?
   Any touchy issues I should be aware of?

10. What messages will provide genuine 'take home' value for this group?
    Should I give them any physical 'take home'? (charts, summaries, etc.)

11. Who is my group 'insider' who can help me in speech development and in getting reliable feedback on my performance?

QUICKIE 18

The beauty of cash

I didn't say the beauty of money. I said cash. Do you realize what a rare and beautiful thing cash is? There are people making $200,000, $300,000, $400,000 a year who haven't seen $1,000 in cash in the past twenty years. It's all plastic, checks and numbers in bank statements. It's never crisp, crunchy, crackly, comely, curvaceous, cold, hard cash.

Well, it is at Mackay Envelope. We give cash to our salespeople for new accounts. When we have our sales meetings we always announce the new accounts, and right there on the spot I pay out a percentage of the value of those accounts to the salespeople, in cash.

By the way, whether it's coin or currency, make sure that your controller or personnel officer is there (as we do) to take careful notes to avoid problems with the IRS.

The place gets very hushed. It's like a church in there when I pull out those bills. I always use brand-new $100 bills. (Mario Puzo, the author of *The Godfather*, calls them, 'honeybees'.) And I count them off, one at a time, 'one, two, three . . .' I'm getting very proficient at making a nice snapping sound. You should see those people. They're intoxicated. They're addicted. They're mesmerized.

I now know that one of the major appeals of gambling is that they pay in cash. Or take the ultimate form of cash: gold. Owning gold was illegal in this country between 1933 and 1975. I know why. The stuff is really habit-forming! People act nutty about it. I'm going to try paying off in those new American eagle coins once or twice and see if they all turn into gold bugs.

QUICKIE 19

The meaning of life

A little song
A little dance
A little seltzer down the pants

— Ted Knight's eulogy to
Chuckles the Clown

Chapter VI

Helping Your Kids Beat The Odds

———◆———

That hostile face staring back at you across the dinner table will someday soon find itself seated across the desk from a potential employer.

You might want to give him or her some idea of what the world is really like before they decide to join the Red Guards and blow it up. I can't promise them that they'll all become millionaires. The odds against that are two hundred to one. And though that might seem like a long shot, this is still the only country that has a million millionaires.

I've had a lot of parents ask me, 'Harvey, you're a successful businessman. You've been around. I want to give Jeff and Janie some advice that will increase the odds of succeeding. What should I say?'

The first thing you have to realize is that you can't tell them very much. The more you gush out advice, the more you'll sound like that old air bag Polonius in *Hamlet*. Be sparing, but when you talk, give them some silver bullets – things that will really make a difference. Here are some thoughts:

DON'T PLAN ON STICKING AROUND JUST TO COLLECT THE GOLD WATCH

Tell them about their first job. Not the one they took to

keep you off their backs or to earn money to buy a car. I mean their first real job. They will be delighted to be making so much money. You must tell them the truth. They are being overpaid.

They are overpaid because they know next to nothing that has any commercial value and have to be trained and gain some experience before they can be of any real value. 'Ridiculous,' they say. 'I'm worth it. Why would they be purposely willing to overpay me?' The answer is, they overpay you for the first two years because they reason that once you know what you're doing, they can underpay you for the next twenty, as, of course, they have to. No company can make money unless they pay out less for their employees than they're charging for the employees' labor.

'Well, then, why does anyone stay around?' they may ask. Because if you can get through that next twenty years and get into a position where you reach the top and help run the place, you'll get overpaid again.

That's the pattern of modern capitalism. You're overpaid while you train, underpaid while you work, but you have the incentive to keep on getting underpaid in hopes you climb to the top, where you can watch other people do the work and get overpaid again for a few years. Obviously, the trick is to see to it that those middle years, the underpaid years, are as few as possible. The way to do that is to recognize that once you've mastered the job, it's time to think about moving on, or up.

If you're working for someone else, as soon as you know what you're doing you'll be making money for that someone else that you could be making for yourself. But if you decide to stay, your real weapon against being underpaid is to realize your ignorance. Recognize that you don't know everything about everything. Challenge yourself, and make yourself learn something new every chance you get.

Do that and you'll be beating the system. Your employer won't be able simply to profit off what you've already learned because you'll be forcing that employer to pay you to learn something new, something commercially valuable, every time you walk into the office. And by the way, if you take that approach, chances are you'll make it to the top a lot more quickly than if you simply lay back and use what you already know.

Would you like to go to a doctor who had taken his last medical course in 1948? Unfortunately, there are still many of them around, but nine tenths of today's medical treatments — lasers, CAT scanners, pacemakers, chemotherapy, drugs — were all developed since the 1948 doctor graduated from med school. You have to keep changing and keep learning so that you are constantly challenging yourself, adding a few new songs to your program every chance you get. If you don't, the world will pass you by. And that's true whether you're an employee or an employer.

FIND SOMETHING YOU LIKE TO DO AND MAKE IT PAY

There is a very unfortunate word in the English language. The name we usually give to work is W-O-R-K. Work isn't work if you like it, but a lot of people seem to think that in order to make a living at something, you shouldn't really enjoy doing it . . . or why would anyone pay you to do it? Not so. Do something you like.

That sounds simpler than it is because so many of us have had childhood experiences in which the people who controlled our lives seemed determined to make us do things we disliked. If that's what our early life was like, it's natural to assume that's what the working world is like, too. It isn't. The world is full of people who are doing what they like to do and making a very good living at it. And it isn't just people in the glamor businesses like advertising, writing, acting and saving the whales. The trick to learn is that if you like something, you can make it pay no matter what business you're in.

I happen to like languages, and I've studied about half a dozen of them. One is Chinese. Now, the truth is that you can make a very good living in my business without being able to speak a word of Chinese. But the superior truth is that you can make an even better living by applying something that seems entirely unrelated, like speaking Chinese, to the envelope business. And you can have a lot more fun.

I used my Chinese speaking ability when I went to China as a leader of a business delegation. The main event, in fact, was reported around the world. I was the first post-World War II American businessman to deliver a speech in Chinese in that country. I made contacts with American businessmen on that trip who started to do business with me, in part because they appreciated my resourcefulness. They didn't know anything about the Chinese language, and they didn't know anything about envelopes either, but apparently they reasoned that someone who took the trouble to learn that difficult language might be the sort of person who knew what he was doing in another area – like manufacturing envelopes.

So by speaking Chinese, I was able to sell a whale of a lot of envelopes. That's putting rule one and rule two together. You don't stick around just to collect the gold watch. You keep changing and learning. And you find something you like and make it work for you – even if it seems totally unrelated to your own business.

MAKE BELIEVE YOUR PARENTS ARE RIGHT SOME OF THE TIME

I was invited to Harvard to address an M.B.A. business seminar a few years ago. After I had given my formal speech to a large roomful of people, they seated me at a table with eight students for a give-and-take session, the kind in which the group can question you very closely and get behind all those glittering generalities you thought you got away with during your speech.

Of course, it works both ways. While they were watching me, I was watching them. What I observed was that every one of those students was, naturally, superbright. But of the eight, there were six you could talk with and two who were incapable of rational conversation. One of the two was belligerent, and the other would ask questions in such a complicated, convoluted way that he might as well have been talking quantum physics instead of business.

As parents you have invested time, money, and agony in trying to get your kids to learn a lot of things they totally dislike. 'Why, why, why do I have to learn to play tennis/eat with a fork/wear socks/study Spanish when I am going to be a nuclear physicist/famous rock star/the richest person in the world?'

It does matter, and not just because there's more to life than what you do for a living. No matter how bright you are or how good you are at what you do, we live in an economy based on change. Capitalism constantly devours its own creations and gives birth to new ones.

Social critics used to describe the brief cycle of products in the marketplace as 'planned obsolescence'. They would wag their fingers at those greedy American corporations that were forever discarding perfectly good old products so they could sell new ones to docile and naïve customers.

Well, you don't hear much about 'planned obsolescence' anymore. The Japanese proved that our problem wasn't too many new products, but too many old, inefficient ones. And the consumers proved that they, not the bloated capitalists, decide what they'll buy – and no amount of hype will sell an inferior, obsolete, or overpriced product.

That pattern of destruction and change is not only repeated over and over again in the marketplace, it also will be an inescapable characteristic of your children's careers.

Unless they are able to *communicate*, to master the basic skills of speaking and writing in a forceful, polite, effective way, the day is likely to come when being a nuclear physicist or an envelopemaker won't be enough. That's because no matter how safe a little niche they may think they have found for themselves, in a world where capitalism constantly destroys its own creations, their jobs will change, so will the skills needed to perform them, and so will the need for them. As a result, not only will they not be able to stick around for the gold watch, they also may have to go out into the hard, cruel world again and market themselves. And unless they can communicate in an attractive fashion, they'll be in big, big trouble.

It's those broad, generalist skills, the ability to communicate in writing, speech, dress, and manners – all those boring things parents and teachers have been driving them nuts about all these years – that someday are going to keep your kids in designer jeans and off the unemployment lines.

THERE'S NO FUTURE IN SAYING IT CAN'T BE DONE

The old saying is that 'If it ain't broke, don't fix it.' The people who make it big are the ones who fix it before it's broke. They force the competition to play catch-up ball. They make their own rules, and the others have to play by them.

A company called TRW has been running an ad in *The Wall Street Journal* that says it beautifully. It shows pictures of a lot of old-timers with impressive titles offering their sage opinions on the great issues of the day.

One of them is Harry Warner. He was president of Warner Brothers in 1927, at the time talking pictures were just coming onscreen. Mr. Warner's comment on this technological breakthrough was: 'Who the hell wants to hear actors talk?' Then there's Robert Millikan, Nobel Prize winner in physics in 1923. He says, 'There is no likelihood man can ever tap the power of the atom.' The best one is

202

from Charles Duell, head of the U.S. Patent Office. In 1899 he said, 'Everything that can be invented, has been invented.' What did all three of these gentlemen have in common? They were completely, dead wrong.

Tell your kids to take chances. The greatest advantage young people have is that without the financial and family encumbrances of older people, they have so little to lose by taking risks. So encourage them to try something new. Defy the odds.

They may fail at times, but to double their success rate you may have to double their failure rate. Just remember: The wheel is tilted in *their* favor, the system is biased on *their* side, because it is based on change. On destroying the old. They have a lot less to lose attempting to make a change than attempting to hang on to an old technology, and to the status quo, in a system that rewards change.

IT'S HARDER TO BE A SUCCESS WHEN YOUR PARENTS ALREADY ARE

There's a saying that goes: 'It's three generations from shirt-sleeves to shirt-sleeves.' What it means is that if your grandparents were poor and your parents become rich and successful, it's a common occurrence that you – your generation – will stumble back into the pattern of your grandparents.

Why? For one thing, nature has an immutable leveling process. No life form keeps improving with every generation. Breeding is an imperfect science. If you don't think so, just look at the families of the presidents of the United States. The same parents who produced Jimmy Carter produced Billy Carter. The same parents who gave us Lyndon Johnson gave us Sam Johnson – whom LBJ kept out of sight in the White House living quarters. And not the least of Richard Nixon's problems was his brother Donald.

We can give our children the right ideals, the right

education, and open doors for them, but the rest is up to them. Every generation finds its own leaders, and it seldom uses the last generation for its castings.

Two years ago, movie actor Kirk Douglas accepted an award from the people in his hometown, Amsterdam, in upstate New York. His son Michael was there and heard his father say, 'I want you to know it was a lot easier for me to become successful than it was for my son. All my dad ever had was a pushcart. If I'd had two pushcarts, I would have been doing twice as well as he did. But Michael made it despite having a famous father, and that takes some doing.'

Your kids don't have to top the old man or Supermom to be a success. If they will set their own goals, use their own special talents and abilities, take what meets their needs from what we have provided for them and discard the rest, they have all they need to be a success by any standard.

Chapter VII

The Closer: How To Succeed

———————— ♦ ————————

You've come a long way with me. Three Harvey Mackay Short Courses and a large packet of Quickies. Now it's time to deal with the big challenge – getting all the way to the top. And I have some ideas on that subject.

Have you noticed that we've gotten this far without overworking the one word that appears in every book of this kind?

The word is determination. A 'how to succeed' book without the obligatory determination scene would be like a Western without a gunfight.

I've been wrestling with how I would meet my determination quota without setting off all the cliché alarms, and I hope I have the answer. I'm going to tell you a couple of stories, Mackay family legends, and let you decide for yourself how important this quality is to your success.

As I've mentioned before, my father was the Associated Press correspondent in St. Paul, and he was damn good at it. The George Will of that era, H. L. Mencken, had nothing to fear from my father as a great stylist. Jack Mackay's greatest professional attribute was his nose for a good story and his indefatigable zeal in getting it.

In 1932, Minneapolis and St. Paul were known as notorious gangster hangouts. There was a kind of an 'open city' policy in effect. At one time or another, John Dillinger, the Barker gang, and Alvin 'Creepy' Karpis – all well-known mobsters of that era – lived in the Twin Cities, more or less unmolested by the police, In return, the gangsters were expected to conduct their business far from the city limits and, of course, to demonstrate their gratitude to the local authorities in a more concrete fashion.

As might be expected, the arrangement broke down. The Barker-Karpis gang kidnaped two wealthy St. Paul residents, banker Edward Bremer and William Hamm, a wealthy brewer. My father covered the subsequent trials for the Associated Press.

On December 16, 1932, an innocent bystander was murdered during the course of an $118,000 Minneapolis bank robbery. The crime was traced to the Barker-Karpis gang, and a police raid on a local poker game netted several characters, including a small-time thief named Leonard Hankins, thought to be a member of the gang. Hankins was convicted of the murder and sentenced to life imprisonment in 1933.

By 1935, most of the Barker-Karpis gang were dead or in prison. As those who survived sought leniency for themselves by publicly accusing each other of various crimes, their stories, dutifully reported by my father, revealed that Hankins had not been involved in the bank robbery/ murder and was not even a member of the gang.

Based on this information, my father persuaded Governor Floyd Olson to begin an investigation, but Olson died before his office could issue a report. His successor lasted only six months and lost a bruising campaign to Harold Stassen, who started again on the Hankins case from ground zero.

By then it was 1939, seven years after the bank robbery and murder. The Stassen report ordering Hankins freed was issued two years later, in 1941, but as my dad wrote, 'Complications set in. There was a 'hold' order on Hankins for a $13 robbery of many years before in Paducah, Kentucky.' Kentucky officials wanted Hankins extradited.

Minnesota authorities, after holding a man for eight

years for a murder of which he was innocent, were not going to compound the inhumane treatment by sending him off to serve time in a southern penitentiary for a $13 crime. Having learned that Kentucky would not accept anyone extradited from a mental asylum, they hit upon the unhappy solution of transferring Hankins to the St. Peter State Hospital for the Criminally Insane.

Throughout, Dad never stopped working on the case and writing about the insanity of holding Hankins, who was perfectly sane, in an insane asylum.

Though Hankins lived a relatively uneventful existence and could purchase a few minor luxuries with the $60 monthly disability pension he received from his World War I service, the nation was preoccupied with World War II, and except for my father's stories and continued pleas for justice, Hankins was forgotten. My father persisted, and finally in 1949 he was able to get some official action.

That year Hankins was certified as sane and was transferred back to the state prison. There was a new round of articles by my dad, and the governor at that time was just starting to get interested when he was appointed to a federal judgeship.

Finally, in 1951, his successor, Governor C. Elmer Anderson, convened an extraordinary session of the state pardon board, the first of its kind in the state, to hear the Hankins case. Two hours before the hearing, the pardon board received official word that the state of Kentucky was 'no longer interested' in Leonard Hankins.

My dad, who had stuck with Hankins throughout, his only advocate, usually his only visitor on Christmas and Thanksgiving, testified at the hearing.

After eighteen long years, ten in a mental institution, Hankins was freed for a crime he did not commit.

Hankin's reward was his freedom. Jack Mackay's was the 'Pall Mall Big Story Award', in which a national radio program presented the award for outstanding work by a journalist. He also received a lifetime supply of Pall Mall cigerettes. Since he had, in his words, 'stopped smoking at the age of eight' after the traditional first cigarette behind the garage, he had no use for his winnings.

That was Jack Mackay. Determination and heart.

Here's another example . . .

During the early 1930's, Governor Olson of Minnesota was a national figure. If he'd had a cryptobiographer as gifted as Robert Penn Warren, author of *All the King's Men*, it would have been Olson as well as Huey Long immortalized as the quintessential depression-era populist governor-*cum*-presidential aspirant.

In the summer of 1935, Olson lay dying of cancer in the Mayo Clinic in Rochester, Minnesota. A deathwatch had developed among reporters, and a competition sprang up among them as to who would be first to have the story.

My father had positioned himself in the street outside Olson's hospital window and had tipped Olson's nurse a few dollars to lower the shade in an adjoining room when Olson succumbed.

Because the hospital would not let the reporters use hospital phones to call in their stories, and since pay phones were much rarer than they are today, my father also had given a boy a quarter to hold a phone for him at a corner grocery store a couple of blocks away.

Olson died, the shade came down, and my father began his run to the grocery store. Just as he was crossing the last street, with all his concentration focused on the national wire service story he would be reporting in the next few minutes, he was hit by a truck. He got up, dusted himself off, limped to the phone, called in his story and only then forced himself to limp back to the hospital and check in. Jack Mackay had his scoop.

It's now twenty-eight years later and I happen to be twenty-eight years old. I had owned my own business for three years, and I was looking for mortgage money to build a new $200,000 manufacturing plant. I went to thirteen different lending institutions, every bank and mortgage company in the Twin Cities. I had the door slammed in my face thirteen times.

Then I took a map and a dime store compass, the kind you use to draw circles, and made a three-inch circle with Minneapolis in the center. I started calling on banks and mortgage companies within the circle. More door slams. I kept drawing circles. Finally I drew a circle big enough to cover Milwaukee, and that's where I got my mortgage money.

Determination? In my father's case, I'm sure he thought he was doing his job and had gotten careless. In my case I didn't regard it as anything more than sound business practice. I'd still be drawing circles today if I hadn't connected. The difference between owning my own land and factory and having someone else put up the building and rent it to me amounted to $1 million.

But even with that kind of money at stake, you'd be surprised how many businesspeople will throw in the towel. Or lie down on the curb. Don't you be one of them.

There *is* a magic formula for success. It's very easy to explain but difficult to execute. Though we all possess *individual* characteristics that make each of us unique, I believe I've seen enough successful people so that I can identify those *shared* characteristics that make successful people successful.

DETERMINATION + GOAL-SETTING + CONCENTRATION = SUCCESS

Gary Player is a South African golfer, winner of dozens of tournaments, including the U.S. Open, Masters, British Open, and PGA. He's a good athlete, but so is everyone else on the tour. Player has had some unusual obstacles to overcome. He's five feet, six inches tall, not exactly a towering figure on the links. He's had major health problems. During the 1960s, he played golf while four bodyguards stood over him. South Africa's racial policies had made Player the object of threats and ugly incidents.

I met Player in 1955 on a practice round the day before the St. Paul Open, which was an important tournament in those days. Player was an unknown professional, and I was an unknown amateur. It was Player's first year on the U.S. tour, and I had just graduated from the University of Minnesota, where I had won my varsity letter in golf, and hadn't yet been talked out of playing professionally.

We hit it off immediately. Since we were in my home-town and we were both about the same age, I offered to show him the sights that evening, such as they were. With about a half dozen other young people, we went off into the night and had a wonderful time. The next day, although my tee-off time was in the afternoon and Player's was in the morning, I was so enthusiastic about my new friend, I decided to walk with him on his round. He had just teed off on the first hole and was heading down the fairway when I reached him. The course was empty. No galleries followed Gary Player in 1955.

'Gary, how you doin' there? Didn't we have a great time last night?' I asked.

He didn't break stride. He didn't turn his head. His eyes stayed focused on the horizon. He had blinders on. His response could have been etched in stone.

'Harvey, I can't talk to you. I must concentrate. I'll see you when I finish.'

I crawled back up to the clubhouse, devastated.

In 1985 I ran into Player, met his wife, and told them the story. She laughed.

'Don't feel bad, Harvey. Actually, he was rather forth-coming with you. He won't even acknowledge my exist-ence when he's on the golf course.'

Determination. Goal-setting. Concentration. All the cliché words. But the clichés are true. That's what makes a winner out of Gary Player, while the rest of us remain duffers, whether at golf or in life.

Perhaps as you read this story, you say to yourself, 'Well, I can do that. I can be just as single-minded and committed as Gary Player.' I put the odds at nine to one that you can't. Let me tell you why.

During the seven-year effort to build the new domed stadium in downtown Minneapolis, I made hundreds of speeches on behalf of the project. I always ended my pitch by asking the audience for a show of hands to indicate how many cared enough about keeping the Twins and Vikings in our community to write their state senators or representatives. Over 90 percent of the audience *always* raised their hands. 'Great,' I said. 'I just want to ask one more thing: Mail me a copy of the letter.' I *never* got more than 10 percent.

Determination? Goal-setting? Concentration? We all think we have them. But the truth is, we don't. I've written this book to help you join that 10 percent club. It's not exclusive. You just have to work to join it.

Peter Ueberroth, the son of an itinerant aluminum-siding salesman, built one of the finest travel companies in the United States and was named *Time's* Man of the Year in January 1985.

I met Ueberroth in the mid-1960s, when he was elected to membership in the Young Presidents' Organization. The YPO is a national business organization made up of presidents, under age fifty, of companies with over seventy-five employees and $5 million in sales. He was an ancient thirty. I had become a member a year earlier.

Ueberroth's sense of self-discipline is so powerful that he can barely stand it when he doesn't find the same quality in others. If he sees an employee speaking with a hand over his mouth, he has been known to reach out and brush it away. He not only has insisted that his employees wear coats and ties at all times, he also has insisted they get new ones if he felt the coats and ties were shabby. And unlike most other clean-desk tyrants, Ueberroth encloses a check for the new clothes with the admonition.

211

Determination? Goal-setting? Concentration? You bet. And Ueberroth has taken it a step farther than Player. Ueberroth is a leader as well as an entrepreneur. He sets the style for others as well as for himself.

Through his efforts, the twenty-third Olympic Games, unlike the twenty-two that preceded it, not only showed a profit, that profit was $215 million. And at the closing ceremonies there was an even more unprecedented event. They gave Ueberroth a standing ovation. I've been to a lot of sporting events in my life, but that was the first time I've ever seen eighty-four thousand people rise to their feet to cheer the person who sold them the ticket.

Curt Carlson is the richest man in my state. He started with nothing, selling premium stamps to grocers during the depression, and built a worldwide conglomerate with sales of over $4 billion annually.

As with Gary Player and Peter Ueberroth, working with Curt is not always a day at the beach. He has been known to chew out his subordinates lavishly. Curt never holds back anything. If you were to put the three of them – Player, Ueberroth, and Carlson – in a room together, give them each an ax, and turn out the lights, I have no doubt that it would be Curt who would walk out of that room – with four axes.

Curt's extra dimension is his vision. He is absolutely fearless when it comes to backing his own judgment. And he will wear no one's harness. Curt wants nothing to do with shareholders, partners, or co-owners. It's all or nothing. Even though he occasionally has sold off bits and pieces of his business, you won't find The Carlson Companies on any exchange. If it means he has to generate all his own capital internally, so be it. Curt would rather go it alone.

Why? It is because he feels his judgment is better than that of his potential shareholders, partners, and co-owners, and he doesn't want them holding him back. During the Carter administration, when we were undergoing a savage recession, Curt shocked me by saying he didn't give a damn what the economy did that year, or the next, as far as his business was concerned. Depression, recession, he couldn't care less about the short term. As usual , the strong would get stronger and the weak would get weaker, and come what may, by 1987, his sales, which were then a little over $1 billion, would be $4 billion.

'You don't say 'whoa' in a horse race,' said Curt. He has been in a horse race his entire life, mostly – because he has left his competition in the dust – with himself. He beat his own deadline by twelve months and 1987 sales were $4 billion. Now his goal is $5 billion.

I think the story that captures him best for me took place the day Minnesota was hit with the worst blizzard in fifty years. Minneapolis-St. Paul International Airport, which is used to dealing with the worst of the worst in weather, was closed for the first time ever. I had scheduled a meeting in New York weeks earlier, and Curt was going there at the same time and had offered me a ride in his jet. Our prospects of getting out of town seemed extremely slim. Finally, though the storm was still pummeling us, the airport inexplicably provided a short grace period and was opened for smaller craft only. Frankly, by that time I wasn't all that keen on thumbing my nose at the Minnesota weather gods, but Curt didn't seem at all concerned. As we were taxiing down the runway to take off, Curt turned to me and said gleefully, 'Look, Harvey, no tracks in the snow!'

Curt Carlson, seventy years old, rich beyond dreams of avarice, could still sparkle with excitement about being first . . . no matter the risk.

No human endeavor with a Gary Player or a Peter Ueberroth or a Curt Carlson in charge will fail. But I have seen business after business go in the tank because owners took their successes for granted.

When I was a kid, a ticket to a University of Minnesota football game was the hottest item in town. And the athletic department knew it. The university's athletic director sneered at the poor people who couldn't get tickets to the Gopher games. The phones were never answered, the lines were long, and the smiles and thank yous were few. They even combed the obituaries for the names of season-ticketholders. University of Minnesota cancellation notices reached the homes of the bereaved about the same time as condolence notes.

When major-league professional sports arrived in the Twin Cities in the early 1960s, the chickens came home to roost. The results of all the badwill the university had generated over the years were realized. The public flocked to the pros, and for twenty-five years, until Lou Holtz arrived, Gopher football was about as popular as jock itch.

No company has a permanent consumer franchise. No one has the only game in town. The never-ending cycle of destruction and change inherent in a capitalist economy always provides new opportunities for those with determination, goals, and concentration.

As long as our world can produce people like Gary Player, Peter Ueberroth, and Curt Carlson, *you* have as good a chance as they did to go all the way to the top.

You don't learn to swim with the sharks in a single outing. High-stakes challenges demand practice and perseverance. This book was written to help you navigate life's risky waters more safely and prosperously. In years to come, someone will undoubtedly update the messages and concepts of this book — with a fresh new slate of role models. I'll bet that several readers of this book will be on that roster of future legends. If you have the will and the spirit, why shouldn't you be one of them?